D0631728

The Basics of
Horseracing

Whitney L. Cobb

Gambling Research Institute

First Printing	*November 1985*
Second Printing	*September 1987*
Third Printing	*October 1988*

Revised Edition

First Printing	*August 1991*

Copyright © 1985, 1991 by Gambling Research Institute
- All Rights Reserved -

ISBN:0-940685-20-5

Library of Congress Catalogue Card Number: 91-70165

Gambling Research Institute (GRI) books are published by Cardoza Publishing, the world's foremost publisher of gambling and gaming books. Write for our free catalogue of gambling books and related gambling items.

CARDOZA PUBLISHING
P.O. Box 1500, Cooper Station
New York, NY 10276
(718)743-5229

Table of Contents

Charts

I. Introduction

Welcome to the fascinating world of horse-racing! Going to the track can be an enjoyable experience in itself, but when you're armed with the knowledge necessary to win at the track, it becomes even more pleasurable. And if you can't make it to the track, legitimate casinos often have race books, and there are race books established in Nevada, as well as Off-Track betting offices in New York.

We'll concentrate on all the factors necessary to understand the sport of racing and how to bet on the thoroughbreds. We'll show you how to read a racing program, past performance charts and the official results of races the way the pros read them. We'll also discuss how to handicap horse races, what to look for in the past performance charts to make you a winner, plus a wealth of other information that will help you beat the races.

Betting and winning, that's the name of the game. We'll show you how to do this in our book.

II. Understanding the Racing Program

We'll be dealing with thoroughbred racing on what are known as **flat tracks.** Thoroughbreds can also be trained as steeplechase runners, but here we're concentrating on those who simply run flat races with a jockey on their backs. Standardbreds, a couple of steps lower in the equine hierarchy, race as trotters and pacers with the rider in a sulky (a light, two wheeled carriage), but thoroughbreds have jockeys who ride directly on their backs.

At all racetracks where thoroughbred racing is going on, programs of that day's racing card are sold. Each race gets a separate page in the program, and gives a wealth of information about the race. The study of the program is the first step a bettor takes when wagering money at the track, but in itself, it is not sufficient to give all the information he needs to make an intelligent bet. That will come from the past performance charts as published in the *Daily Racing Form.*

Chart 1
Santa Anita: 6th Race, 1/31/85

PICK SIX RACE

	WIN	PLACE	SHOW	NO.

6 FURLONGS

About 1,200 Meters

6 TH RACE

FRIENDLY HILLS WOMAN'S CLUB

PURSE $21,000. For maidens four years old and upward. Four-year-olds, 117 lbs.; older, 118 lbs.

Track Record—CHINOOK PASS (3) 120 lbs. December 26, 1982 1:07⅗

MAKE SELECTION BY PROGRAM NUMBER — PROBABLE ODDS

OWNER	TRAINER	JOCKEY
Longden & Carr Stables	John Longden	10
White purple sash, sleeves and cap		William
1 BILLIKIN 117		Shoemaker
Ch.c.81, Vice Regent—Alibi 4th		
Coelho & Valenti	J. R. McCutcheon	30
Orange, black cap		Frank
2 DAIRYDON 117		Olivares
Br.c.81, Don B.—Unreachable Star		
Summa Stable (Lessee)	George W. Scott	12
Blue, silver coin on back, silver bar on sleeves, blue and silver cap		Gary
3 COMMANDER'S SONG 117		Stevens
Ch.c.81, Dust Commander—Char Song		
George Putnam	R. W. Mulhall	15
Red, black and silver sashes and coat-of-arms, red, black and silver cap		Dario
4 BLAME THE DUKE *112		Lozoya
Ch.c.81, Petit Duc—Blame The Apple		
Allen E. Paulson	Gary Jones	4
White, blue and red emblem, white stars on blue sleeves, red cuffs, blue and red cap		Sandy
5 KINETIC 117		Hawley
B.c.81, Vitriolic—Denim Doll		
Universal Stable	D. Wayne Lukas	2
Yellow, blue diamond stripes, yellow sleeves, yellow and blue cap		Patrick
6 LION OF THE DESERT 117		Valenzuela
Ch.c.81, Alydar—Azeez		
G. V. D. V. Thoroughbred Farm	John Canty	30
White, black horseshoe, green "GVDV" on back, white bars and cuffs on green sleeves, green and white cap		Alex
7 SAINT CADVAN 117		Fernandez
Br.c.81, Bold Reason—Mittle Maid		
Roy L. Tyra	James Jordan	20
Pink, black dots, pink and black cap		Chris
8 COWBOY ROMAN 117		Lamance
Ch.c.81, Spicey Roman—No More Bells		
Elmendorf Farm, Inc.	Gary Jones	3
Burgundy, gold sash and cap		Chris
9 SUN MASTER 117		McCarron
B.c.81, Foolish Pleasure—Sunny Today		
Wild Plum Farm & Whitham	Mary Lou Tuck	6
Orange, white blocks on back, white cap		Terry
10 BECAUSE IT'S TRUE 117		Lipham
Br.c.81, Believe It—Big Rhapsody		

(★) 5 LBS. APPRENTICE ALLOWANCE CLAIMED

EQUIPMENT CHANGE—Lion Of The Desert races without blinkers.

Copyright © 1985, by DAILY RACING FORM, INC.
Reprinted with permission of copyright owner.

However, without the racing program, the bettor will be in the dark about a number of things that are extremely important to him or her, and in this chapter we'll show just how much one can learn from a racing program.

With this purpose in mind, we're going to examine the program for the 6th Race of January 31, 1985 at Santa Anita Race Track, which is located in Southern California, about thirty miles east of Los Angeles.

Looking at this page, we see the *card* for the 6th race of the day, called the ***Friendly Hills Woman's Club***. Often tracks name races after organizations so that the members of that organization will be well represented at the racetrack that day. It makes for good public relations.

At the very top of the program page we see the term ***Pick Six Race***. This is a gimmick kind of bet in which a bettor must pick the winners of six consecutive races to qualify for an enormous prize. It's very difficult to do, and sometimes days go by without anyone doing it. This has nothing to do with this race, so let's disregard it.

What is important is knowing the distance of the race. This is shown in the diagram in the upper left hand corner; it's a 6 furlong race. **Furlong** is an old English term signifying what was the length of a furrow in farming. But now it's standardized at 220 yards, or 1/8 of a mile. There are 8 furlongs to a mile, and thus, a 6 furlong race is 3/4 of a mile.

Since most thoroughbreds are built and bred for speed, the 6 furlong distance is the most frequently run of all distances, and is the test of the sprinter.

The little black arrow on the top of the diagram shows where the race will begin, and the line across the track of the diagram shows where it will end. A gate is placed where the arrow is located, and all the horses will come out of the gate when they begin their run. They'll finish their race right in front of the grandstand, where the spectators and bettors stay.

Next we discover that the race is for a **purse** of $21,000 and is for maidens. **Maidens** are horses that have never won a race before, and these horses, being four years old and upward, have been running a while without winning a race, since thoroughbreds generally start racing for purses at the age of 2.

All of the four year olds will be assigned a **weight** of 117 pounds; older horses will get 118 pounds. Older horses, being stronger, are penalized slightly for their age.

Then we see the track record for this distance at Santa Anita. It is held by Chinook Pass, who as a three-year-old carrying 120 pounds, ran six furlongs on December 26, 1982 in 1:07-3/5; that is in one minute seven and 3/5 seconds. All fractions of seconds at racetracks are in fifths of seconds, there thus being five fifths to every second when counted as a fraction. The time of 1:07-3/5 is extremely fast, even for a speed track like Santa Anita.

Under this we see "Make Selection By Program Number." At a racetrack, the correct way to bet on a horse is by his program number. If we wanted to bet on the number 1 horse, Billikin, we'd say "$2 to win on number 1," without mentioning the horse's name. When betting at Off-Track Betting parlors in

New York, each horse is assigned a letter instead of a number. At legitimate race books, where there aren't track programs always available, then one might bet using the horse's name.

Now, let's examine the other information available on this program.

Each horse listed has the following information shown next to his name. His owners, his trainer, his jockey, his jockey's colors, his color, the year of his birth, his sire, his dam, the weight the jockey is carrying and the morning line odds. Let's examine these by showing this information on Billikin, the number 1 horse.

Billikin's owners are the Longden & Carr Stables, and his trainer is Johnny Longden, who was one of the legendary jockeys in his day and is now, like many other aging former jockeys, a trainer.

Sometimes knowing the stables that own the horse and the trainer who trains him is important information. Records are kept on the trainer's winning records, and some owners are always trying to win with their horses, while others have lackluster records. Knowing which trainers are competent, and which owners are trying is information that takes time to find out, but astute bettors make it their business to find out these facts.

Next we come to the colors worn by the jockey. In this case Billikin's jockey will be wearing a white purple sash, sleeves and cap. Track announcers follow the progress of horses around a track during a race by colors rather than numbers oftentimes, and it's easy to follow the horse's progress from the grandstand if you key in on his colors.

The horse's color is stated below his name. Billikin is a chestnut colt (Ch.c) born in 1981, which makes him a four-year-old. His sire was Vice Regent and his dam was Alibi 4th. **Sire** in racing terms means father and **dam** is the mother. For this race he is carrying 117 pounds, and his jockey is William Shoemaker, one of the greatest jockeys who has ever ridden horses. Shoemaker is still riding in his 50s, and holds the record for most wins by a jockey for all time.

The morning line odds on Billikin is 10-1. Morning line odds aren't the actual odds on the horse, but only those suggested by the track linemaker. The actual odds will be determined by the racing and betting public, whose bets will be computed by totalizer (totes or mutuels) and will eventually set the correct odds based on money bet on each horse.

The morning line odds, however, give the racegoer an idea of how the track handicapper sees the chance of each horse in this race. The morning line *favorite* is the number 6 horse, Lion of the Desert, who is 2-1, and the second choice is Sun Master, the number 9 horse.

Astute bettors watch the wagering to see how close the final odds are to the morning line odds. If there's a big discrepancy, they take note of this fact. For example, if a horse is 12-1 on the morning line and is bet down to 3-1, obviously heavy money is coming in from somewhere. And the converse is true. If a horse is 3-1 on the morning line and goes off at 7-1, then insiders know that the horse's condition might not be that great. These aren't infallible methods to spot winners and losers, but they should be weighed, along with other factors.

All the horses in this 6th race are **colts**, that is, male horses under five years of age. They all carry the same weight, 117 pounds, except for Blame the Duke, the number 4 horse, who gets in at 112, because its jockey is an apprentice, and is entitled to a 5 pounds allowance. When Dario Lozoya, the jockey, wins enough races, he loses his *bug* and the mounts he gets won't be entitled to that allowance anymore.

There's also one equipment change in the race. Lion of the Desert will be racing without blinkers. If he's been racing with blinkers steadily, then this change may be meaningful, and after the race, the serious horseplayer should make a note to that effect.

When at a racetrack, be sure to purchase the track's program and to study the information listed. Some of the facts, such as the program number of the horse, is necessary to know in order to bet correctly on that horse. Other information, taken together with the past performance charts, will give the bettor a solid understanding of the horses in the race as well as the conditions relevant to that particular race. Too many bettors disregard the program information, except to find out the number of the horses, but you shouldn't make this mistake.

III. The Bets

In this section, we'll discuss the principal types of wagers that can be made at the track, OTB or a racing book in Nevada.

Win, Place and Show Bets

These are the most popular bets made by the racing public. If a bet is made ($2 minimum) that a horse will **win** the race, that horse must come in first for the bettor to win his or her bet.

If a bet is made for second, or **place**, and the horse finishes in first or second, then the bettor wins his or her wager.

If a bet is made for **show**, or third, and the horse finishes in first, second of third (*in the money*), then the bettor wins.

Payoffs for this type of betting may look like this:

Chart 2
Sample Payoffs: Win, Place and Show

$2 Mutuel Prices:	8 Winning Horse	6.00	3.80	3.20
	6 Second Horse		13.20	5.40
	12 Third Horse			2.80

Only those who have bet the number 8 horse to win would get the $6 payoff. The winning horse went off at 2-1, and the $6 payoff represents $4 at 2-1 and the original $2 bet, for a total of $6. Those who bet for place would get the $3.80 payoff, and those betting show would collect $3.20.

The second horse was a longshot, with a big payoff for place and show, and any bet on this horse for second or third would receive a payoff, but those who bet it to win would lose their bet. The third horse would reward its backers only if they made show bets. For example, if the third horse were bet for win or place, those would be losing bets. Only the show bets, for third, would be paid off.

Daily Double

In order to entice the betting public to attend all the races and arrive early, tracks offer **daily double** betting, which is picking the winner of the first and the second races. A bettor must pick both to get a payoff. Bets on the daily double are at a minimum of $2.

The payoff would look like this:

> **$2 Daily Double 4-11 paid $39.20.**

Since horses at a track are bet on by program number, the number 4 horse won the first race, and the number 11 horse won the second race for this $39.20 payoff.

Exacta Betting

To win an **exacta**, a bettor must pick the horses that finish first and second in the exact order.

At many tracks, only $5 minimum exacta betting is permitted, though at other tracks there are $2.00 exacta bets allowed. The payoff would look like this:

> **$5 Exacta 10-3 paid $215.50.**

Again, horses are bet by program number rather than by name, and the payoffs reflect this.

Quinella Betting

In **quinella** betting, the player has to pick the first two finishers of the race, but not in correct order, just the winner and place horse. These wagers can be made for as little as $2. A typical payoff would look like this:

> **2 Quinella 8-1 paid $35.60.**

Sometimes quinella and exacta betting is allowed in the same race. Then a payoff would look like this:

> **$2 Quinella 9-4 paid $39.00 $2 Exacta 4-9 paid $93.40.**

The exact order of finish was 4 and 9 as reflected by the exacta payoff, which is higher than the quinella payoff because of the level of difficulty in picking the first and second horses finishing in exact order rather than just picking the first two finishers in any order.

There are a number of **gimmick** bets available at different tracks, with very high and exotic payoffs, but the chances of winning these decrease in proportion to the payoffs. Sometimes these are called triples pick six, twin doubles and the most exotic pick nine, in which a player must pick all nine winners to receive the ultimate prize.

We'd suggest that the readers stick to the bets mentioned in this section. Some give good payoffs, and once your handicapping skills are perfected, you can try for other more exotic types of bets.

Payoffs on Winning Bets

It is often difficult for beginners to figure out the correct payoffs for winning bets when the horse they backed comes in first. This is because payoffs are calculated to $2, not $1, and the $2 bet is added to the total. For example, at 3-1, a winning bet would pay off not only the $6 (3-1 x $2) but the original $2 bet as well, for a payoff of $8. The payoff might be a little higher, for the horse might have gone off at 3.20-1 and in this case the payoff would be $8.40. But tote boards at tracks show the odds closest to even numbers, and not those in between. Use the following guide for winning payoffs at a track, the OTB or a race book. All are calculated for $2 bets.

Chart 3
Payoffs on Winning Bets

Odds	Payoff
1-5	$ 2.40
2-5	2.80
3-5	3.20
4-5	3.60
Even (1-1)	4.00
6-5	4.40
7-5	4.80
8-5	5.20
9-5	5.60
2-1	6.00
5-2	7.00
3.1	8.00
7-2	9.00
4-1	10.00
9-2	11.00
5-1	12.00
6-1	14.00
7-1	16.00
8-1	18.00
9-1	20.00
10-1	22.00
15-1	32.00
20-1	42.00
25-1	52.00
30-1	62.00
40-1	82.00
50-1	102.00
60-1	122.00
70-1	142.00
80-1	162.00
90-1	182.00

Usually, tote boards will only go up to 99-1. However, a 99-1 shot on a tote board may very well pay over 100-1.

The higher the odds, the more the likelihood is that the payoff won't be exactly what is shown on this table, but may be higher. For example, a tote board will show odds of 50-1 with the next increment at 55-1 and will not show the exact 54-1 odds that the horse will go off at. In this example, the payoff would be $110 for a $2 ticket instead of $102.

Always remember to add on the original $2 bet when figuring the payout. If you bet more than $2 simply multiply the payoffs by the amount bet, using $2 as the base. For example, if you bet $10 on a 4-1 shot, your payoff would be 5 times the payoff for a $2 bet, or $50.

IV. Five Principal Types of Races

The standard is generally nine races per day at most tracks in the country. Of the nine races per day, most will be claiming races, and there generally will be one feature race which will be either a handicap or a stakes race. The others may be allowance or maiden races. We'll look at each one in order of purse values, with the most lucrative first.

Stakes Races

The top horses are run in **stakes races**, which are the most lucrative of all races, paying the most money to those horses finishing in the money. In these races, the owners of the horses entered put up money, and the racing association or track contributes more money.

For example, the Kentucky Derby, the most famous of all the races run in America, is a stakes race. To enter a horse in this race, the owner must first pay a nominating fee, then other payments up to the time of the running of the race in May of each year.

In addition, the track, Churchill Downs, itself puts up money, which is known as **added** money. This race is the premier race for three-year-olds in America, and is followed by more people with greater interest than any other race. Together with the Preakness and the Belmont Stakes, the Kentucky Derby forms the Triple Crown of racing, the most sought after honor by owners of thoroughbreds. Very few have won the triple crown, but the names of horses like Whirlaway, Count Fleet, Citation, Seattle Slew and Secretariat will always be immortalized because they won the Triple Crown.

There are stakes races for two-year-olds and also for older horses, and some great horses, such as Kelso and John Henry, both **geldings**, that is, male horses that have been unsexed, competed long after other horses were retired to stud, and won fortunes in money for their owners.

Handicap Races

These are the next best money races for horses, and attract top fields of class horses. The weight each horse must carry in the race is assigned separately by the official handicapper at the track so that each of the horses has a chance at winning the race. For example, the horse with the best record, with the most class, gets *top weight* and then other horses, according to their records, get lesser weight. The weakest horse in a handicap event will have the least weight. For example, the top horse may be assigned 126 pounds, while the weakest horse may be assigned ten pounds less.

However, with top horses, added weight is often not sufficient to stop them, and handicapping horses by weight alone is not a sure way to equalize their chances in a particular race. Often, the best horse is given so much weight by a particular handicapper that he is *scratched*, or withdrawn from the race, because of the punishing burden of carrying all that weight.

Horses, especially thoroughbreds, are powerful animals, but they have been bred for certain traits, such as speed, and with too much weight, they are subject to injuries to their legs. Owners of great horses don't want to take the chance of having their horses break down during a race because of added weight on their backs.

Allowance Races

In an **allowance race**, the weights carried by each of the horses are generally set arbitrarily according to the number of races run or amount of money won by each horse entered. For example, in a race for three-year-olds and up (older), the three-year-olds may be assigned a weight of 117 pounds, while all older horses will be assigned 122 pounds.

Allowance races attract horses which aren't of the caliber of stakes or handicap racehorses, but are too valuable to be entered in claiming races, in which the owners may lose their particular horse to another owner.

Since allowance races are run for different amounts of prize money, there are various purses offered for these races. A horse running in an allowance race for a $10,000 purse at a smaller track will be definitely moving up in class if he is entered in an allowance race at a major track for $25,000. And so on, up or down. In the past performance charts, a bettor can see just what kind of race the horse he is thinking of betting on has been used to running. A stakes horse who is entered in an allowance race is definitely going down in class. Often stake horses are entered in allowance races after a long layoff, to give them a race under their belt before attacking the stake races again.

Maiden Races

These are races for valuable horses who haven't yet won a race, and are a cut above claiming races. There is a special category of Maiden Race, called *Maiden Special Weight*, for two-year-old horses who haven't yet won. Often the very best of future stakes winners start their careers in these races, and once they've *broken their maiden*, they move on to stakes races.

Anytime you see a Maiden Race listed, you know the horses entered haven't won a race before, or, if they've won before, it would be a wholly different kind of race, such as a steeplechase, while this race is on a flat dirt or turf (grass) field.

Claiming Races

These are the most frequent kind of races a bettor will encounter at the racetrack. The horses in these races are the bottom of the barrel as far as racing is concerned. The claiming races are the cheapest in terms of purses and horses, of all races at the track.

These cheap races attract basically three different kinds of horses. There are those horses who are moving up in class, and will go from a *claimer* of $5,000 (in which they can be claimed for that sum) to a $6,000 claimer.

Let's explain what is meant by *claiming* at this time. Any horse entered in a claiming race can be claimed or taken away for the claiming price mentioned in the program, by either another owner who has raced horses at that track, or, in unusual cases at some tracks, by anyone who wants to claim the horse.

Other owners who wish to claim a horse must do so prior to the race, not afterwards, in writing. Once a horse is claimed, the new owner runs all the risks of the horse in that race. Should the horse be seriously injured or even have to be destroyed, the claimant is still stuck with that horse.

The purse belongs to the previous owner, however. The official charts of the race will show which horses, if any, have been claimed, and by whom. Usually the claiming owner knows something about the horse; that's why he or she is claiming it. However, often an *also-ran*, a horse finishing out of the money, is claimed.

The second category is a horse moving down in class, going from a $7,500 claimer down to $6,000.

These horses are rapidly going down in class, as their owners desperately try to unload them, since horses are expensive animals to feed and take care of. Or the owner is trying to find a level in which he can win a share of the purse to pay for feed, etc.

The third category is horses of mediocre talent who have no value in stud, and plod along, year after year, racing in claimers, with their owners trying to pick up a few bucks here and there, or unload a horse now and then. Very few horses entered in claimers are claimed by other owners, but the system is very effective in preventing owners from trying to steal a race from weaker horses by entering their horse in a cheap claiming race.

If the horse wins the race, but is claimed, then the owner loses out in the long run, giving up a fine horse just to grab a cheap purse. Claiming races involving cheaper horses, often known as *platers*, make up many of the gimmick races in which daily doubles and triples and exacta betting is allowed. With cheap horses, without consistency and class, it is often difficult to handicap the winner of one of those claiming races.

The cheaper races attract weaker and more inconsistent horses, while the handicap and stakes races attract the best and most consistent horses. Form, as measured by past performance, is more relevant in the better type races.

V. The Daily Racing Form

In order to properly handicap races, the *Racing Form* is a must. At one time it competed with the *Morning Telegraph*, but it's been many years since the *Telegraph* went out of business, and now the *Racing Form* has the field all to itself.

The *Racing Form* covers all the major tracks running in America, so that, with one issue, you can bet or at least handicap races wherever they're run.

The daily newspaper is devoted only to racing, and there's a wealth of information here for the person interested in betting on the ponies. Its main function, however, is showing the past performances of all horses running in all the races.

Only the *Racing Form* has this past performance information, and it is from these past performances that one is able to handicap races.

Each issue contains an explanation of all the information described in a past performance chart. It looks like this:

Chart 4
Daily Racing Form:
Understanding Past Performance Charts

Copyright © 1985, by DAILY RACING FORM, INC.
Reprinted with permission of copyright owner.

There is a wealth of information available in the past performance charts. Some handicappers look for only particular factors to study, others look at the whole chart. But whatever a handicapper wants can be found here. It can be said without contradiction that, for the vast majority of horseplayers, the past performance charts are the most important tool they have in figuring out the outcome of a race.

Past Performance Charts

Let's now examine the charts for the horses entered in the 7th race at Saratoga for Thursday, August 15th, 1985. Before we look at the horses' records, let's first study just what kind of race this is, and the distance.

The race is at a distance of 6 furlongs (3/4 of a mile), a sprint. The record for this distance at Saratoga is 1:08 minutes, as we can see in the parentheses right after the distance of the race, 6 furlongs, is mentioned.

This particular race is an Allowance Race, which means that the horses are better than those entered in Claiming Races, and not of the caliber of horses in a Stakes or Handicap Race. The purse is $36,000, which is divided among the first four finishers.

The race is for three-year-olds and upward which have not won a race of $16,500 since January 1st. Then there are the weights assigned to each horse. All 3-year-olds are first assigned 117 pounds, while older horses are assigned 122 pounds. However, non-winners of two races of $15,000 since July 1st are allowed 3 pounds, and since January 1st are allowed 5 pounds. And non-winners of races of $16,500 in 1984-85 are allowed 7 pounds.

That's why each horse will have different weights assigned to it. Loud and Clear will have 115 pounds, Whoop Up 110 pounds (the small 7 next to the weight indicates that it has an apprentice jockey allowance of 7 pounds), Faces Up and Majestic Venture will have 115 pounds, and, along with Mayanesian, will have the top weight in this race.

The two important things that the past perform-ance charts don't show are the name of the jockey riding the horse and the morning line odds. This information will have to come from the program at the track, or, if betting at a casino or legitimate sports book, they'll have this information posted prior to post time.

Not only does the bettor find out about the past performances of each horse, but there is information about his breeding as well as the color of the horse. Loud and Clear's *sire* (father) was Stop the Music. His *dam* (mother) was Go To Bed, and her sire was Cohoes.

Breeding can be important, but must be researched carefully. Some horses are bred for speed, some for endurance, others for both speed and endurance. Knowledge of the habits of the sires and mares is important in this regard. In a 6 furlong race, which is just a sprint, speed is the main factor, not endurance, while in a race of a mile or over, endurance becomes a prime factor.

We see that Loud and Clear is a dark bay or brown colt (c.) 4 years old. In 1985 he ran one time

Chart 5

Past Performance Chart—7th Saratoga, 8/15/85

DAILY RACING FORM, THURSDAY, AUGUST 15, 1985

7th Saratoga

6 FURLONGS. (1.08) ALLOWANCE. Purse $36,000. 3-year-olds and upward which have not won a race of $16,500 since January 1. Weights, 3-year-olds, 117 lbs. Older, 122 lbs. Non-winners of two races of $15,000 since July 1, allowed 3 lbs. Of two such races since January 1, 5 lbs. Of two races of $16,500 in 1984–85, 7 lbs. (Maiden, claiming, starter and state-bred races not considered.)

Loud And Clear

Own.—Keewaydin Stable **115**

Dk. b. or br. c. 4, by Stop The Music—Go To Bed, by Cohoes
Br.—Snowden H & H Jr (Ky)
Tr.—Veitch Sylvester E
Lifetime 6 3 1 1 $44,600

1985	1	1	0	0	$15,000
1984	3	2	0	0	$22,800

5Aug85-7Sar 6f :22⁴ :45³ 1:10¹ft 2½ 117 2½ 1hd 1² 1¹¾ Cruguet J¹ Aw25000 89-16 LoudAndClear,SilverSlate,Sardowic 7

25Aug84-3Sar 7f :23 :46³ 1:23³ft 3½ 117 4³ 4²½ 3² 1²¼ Cruguet J⁶ Aw20000 84-18 LoudAndCler,Mgicus,SteppinBttler 8

10Aug84-2Sar 6f :22¹ :45³ 1:10¹ft 4½ 117 2hd 1½ 1⁴ 1⁵¾ Day P⁶ Mdn 89-13 Loud And Clear, Solidified, Incite 14

15Jly84-6Bel 6f :22⁴ :46⁴ 1:11²ft 3½e116 7⁴ 12¹³10¹¹10¹⁰½ Fann B⁴ Mdn 74-17 KeyToTheFlg,Duomo,CoolWelcom 12

9Oct83-4Bel 6f :22² :45 1:11 ft 3½ 118 5⁵ 6¹¹ 3⁹½ 3⁵¼ Fell J⁶ Mdn 82-10 UpperStar,ForHalo,LoudArdClear 11

29Sep83-4Bel 6f :22⁴ :46¹ 1:11²ft 41 118 2hd 1hd 2½ 2²¼ Maple E² Mdn 83-17 CountryMnor,LoudAndClr,MlTickt 13

Aug 14 Sar 3f ft :39 b Aug 10 Sar 5f ft 1:04 b Aug 3 Sar 3f ft :38 b ● Jly 26 Bel 5f sy 1:00 h

Whoop Up

Own.—Edwards R L **110⁷**

Ch. h. 5, by Divine Royalty—Balanced Melody, by Balance Of Power
Br.—Edwards R L (Wash)
Tr.—Nesky Kenneth A
Lifetime 24 4 3 6 $95,510

1985	8	1	2	3	$36,950
1984	16	3	1	3	$58,560
Turf	3	1	0	0	$19,800

7Aug85-6Sar 1 Ⓣ:46³1:11 1:36²fm 16 108⁷ 1² 1¹½ 2⁴ 5⁷½ Wynter N A³ Aw40000 86-14 JudgeCosta,FearlessLeder,Sondrio 10

14Jly85-6Bel 7f :22³ :45⁴ 1:23²ft 2½ 110⁷ 1²½ 1² 1⁵ 1³¾ Guerra A A³ Aw27000 85-21 WhoopUp,GoldenImmigrnt,SirLedr 6

1Jun85-8Pim 5f :22¹ :45² :57²ft 4¼ 116 1½ 1hd 3½ 2²¼ KupfrTJ⁵ Mister Diz H 96-17 Prince Valid, Whoop Up, Ryburn 7

25May85-6Pim 5f :22¹ :45² :57³ft 4½ 117 1½ 2hd 3nk 2nk † Pino M G⁵ Aw22000 97-12 Ryburn, ‡Whoop Up, Prince Valid 7

†25May85—Disqualified and placed third; Bore in

15Feb85-7Aqu 6f ⊡:22³ :46 1:11¹ft 3½ 110⁷ 1½ 1¹ 2hd 2¹½ Guerra A A⁶ Aw25000 87-26 Mt.Livermor,WhoopUp,Coopr'sHwk 7

27Jan85-8Aqu 6f ⊡:22¹ :45²1:10¹ft 18 114 2¹ 4⁵ 5¹⁰ 5¹⁰¾ Samyn J L⁵ Coaltown 82-20 Entropy, Muskoka Wyck,MainStem 6

11Jan85-8Aqu 6f ⊡:23¹ :47¹1:11³ft 2½ 110⁷ 1¹ 2hd 3¹ 3⁴¾ Guerra A A² Aw25000 81-30 EcsttcPrd,BlndMn'sBlff,WhoopUp 6

1Jan85-7Aqu 6f ⊡:21⁴ :44³1:09³ft 6½ 110⁷ 1² 1¹ 2½ 3²½ Guerra A A⁶ Aw25000 93-13 StoneyLonsom,GrtHuntr,WhoopUp 6

Aug 3 Sar 5f ft :59 h Jly 28 Aqu 4f ft :48² h Jly 22 Aqu 5f gd 1:02¹ b (d) ● Jly 10 Aqu 5f ft 1:00 h

The Wedding Guest

Own.—Harris C E **110⁷**

B. c. 4, by Hold Your Peace—Ancient Miss, by Olden Times
Br.—Ionian Farm (Fla)
Tr.—Jolley Leroy Jr
Lifetime 18 6 2 1 $194,386

1985	7	2	1	0	$31,320
1984	10	4	1	1	$162,666
Turf	1	0	0	0	

3Aug85-1Sar 7f :22 :44¹ 1:21¹ft 8¼ 115 1½ 1¹ 2² 2³¾ Velez R I³ Aw36000 92-11 KnghtfArmr,ThWddngGst,BBOfSts 7

30Jun85-7Bel 6f Ⓣ:21⁴ :44³1:09²fm 7½ 117 3³ 3³ 4⁵ 5⁸ Cruguet J⁶ Aw36000 85-18 Alev, Equalize, River Demcn 6

14Apr85-8Aqu 6f :22² :45 1:08⁴ft 4½e123 3²½ 5⁴ 6¹¹ 6¹³¼ VasquezJ¹ Bold Ruler 84-22 RockyMrrige,Entropy,MjesticVntur 6

14Apr85—Grade II

19Mar85-9Hia 6f :21⁴ :44⁴ 1:09 ft *1 119 2² 2½ 1⁴ 1⁴ Vasquez J¹ Aw17000 96-13 ThWddngGst,NrthrnOcn,‡FrndlBb 11

20Feb85-9GP 7f :22¹ :44³ 1:22²ft 5¾ 115 1²½ 1³ 2¹½ 6¹⁰ GurrWA⁶ Ft Laud'le H 82-23 For Halo, Bright Ivor, Jim Bracken 6

7Feb85-9GP 7f :22⁴ :45¹ 1:23 ft 3 115 1¹½ 1¹½ 1²½ 1¾ Guerra W A⁵ Aw21200 89-32 TheWeddingGuest,BrightIvor,Bllo 10

12Jan85-9GP 6f :21⁴ :45 1:09³ft 5 114 2½ 3¹½ 4³½ 6⁷¼ GurrWA² Hallandale H 84-16 ForHlo,NorthernTrdr,Rupr't'sWing 11

25Nov84-8Aqu 6f :22 :45³ 1:10⁴ft 14e112 4³ 7⁷½10⁵¾10⁵¾ VelsquzJ¹ Sport Pg H 81-25 Trntr,MuskokWyck,NewConnction 13

25Nov84—Grade III

Aug 12 Bel 4f ft :49 b ● Aug 1 Bel 5f ft 1:00² h Jly 28 Bel 5f ft 1:02² b Jly 25 Bel 4f ft :51⁴ b

Copyright © 1985, by DAILY RACING FORM, INC.
Reprinted with permission of copyright owner.

River Demon

Own.—Thieriot C Mrs — 1087

B. c. 4, by Riverman—Lycabette, by Lyphard
Br.—Thieriot Mrs C H (Ky)
Tr.—Cantey Joseph B
Lifetime 13 4 3 3 $78,320

1985	9	3	1	3	$57,940
1984	4	1	2	0	$20,380
Turf	2	0	0	2	$8,640

19Jly85-7Bel	6f	Ⓣ:212	:442	1:094fm	*8-5	115	1½	12	1hd	31¾	McCarron G2	Aw36000	89-14	ZanyTactics,Maynesin,RiverDemon	6
30Jun85-7Bel	6f	Ⓣ:214	:443	1:092fm	2	117	11½	13	11½	31½	McCarron G1	Aw36000	91-18	Alev, Equalize, River Demcn	6
16Jun85-7Bel	7f	:222	:444	1:23 m	*6-5	117	11½	11½	1½	35¼	McCarron G1	Aw36000	82-17	Alev, Alchise, River Demor	4
6Jun85-8Bel	6f	:221	:444	1:102gd	3	110	11½	12½	14	2hd	McCarron G4	HcpO	90-15	Basket Weave, River Demcn, Alev	7
27Mar85-9OP	6f	:221	:451	1:093gd	*3-2	121	12½	12½	13	19½	Whited D E3	Aw18000	92-25	River Demon, Beat 'EmUp,Matsaco	6
8Mar85-9OP	6f	:212	:453	1:102ft	*4-5	121	2½	21	68	716	McCarron G7	Aw18000	72-22	T. H. Bend, SafeCracker,Lauri'sLad	7
16Feb85-9OP	6f	:212	:442	1:093ft	4¼	115	1½	2hd	57	518¼	WtdDE5	Hot Spring H	74-16	Tylor'sSpecil,TemerityPrinc,Mtsco	5
16Feb85—Was wide															
8Feb85-7OP	5½f	:222	:452	1:033gd	*2-3	121	11½	11½	12	11½	Snyder L4	Aw18000	95-11	RiverDemon,PssingBse,RueDLChnc	9

Aug 6 Sar 5f ft 1:023 b   Jly 14 Bel 5f ft :593 h

Cut Away

Own.—Allen H — 115

B. h. 6, by Cutlass—Jaidan, by Jaipur
Br.—Early Bird Stud (Fla)
Tr.—Jacobs Eugene
Lifetime 38 5 7 3 $135,563

1985	1	0	0	0	
1984	17	2	3	0	$57,978
Turf	4	0	1	0	$3,570

13Jly85-7Bel	6½f	:224	:454	1:164ft	17	111	42½	32	513	517½	Cruguet J5	HcpO	74-19	TnRogrsFor,BsktWv,KnghtofArmor	5
7Nov84-7Hol	1	:45	1:10	1:36 ft	11e	113	31	1hd	13½	14	Hawley S10	HcpO	— —	CutAway,PrairieBreker,FbulousDd	11
14Oct84-7Bel	7f	:224	:454	1:241ft	11	115	51½	74½	79½	79	Cruguet J1	Aw33000	72-28	North Glade, Puntivo, Tenifly	7
6Oct84-7Bel	6f	:223	:454	1:103ft	11	115	53¼	53¼	52¾	4½	Cruguet J3	Aw33000	88-17	UpPpsAwnnr,I'mARndr,NrthrnTrdr	8
23Sep84-8Bel	6f	:221	:453	1:101ft	48	121	108¼	96¾	87¾	99½	CruguetJ9	Fall Hiwt H	81-19	Mmison,TimelssNtiv,MuskokWyck	12
23Sep84—Grade II; Broke slowly															
25Aug84-7Sar	6f	:221	:451	1:10 ft	3¾	117	43½	46	55¼	58¼	Pincay L Jr1	Aw33000	82-18	MjesticVenture,SonrieJorge,Dipson	9
18Aug84-5Sar	7f	:221	:444	1:221ft	3½	117	22	21½	15	1¾	Cordero AJr3	Aw23000	91-15	Cut Away, Dancing Crown, A Gift	7
5Aug84-6Sar	6f	:22	:443	1:093ft	12	1125	54	53¾	53	45½	Ward W A6	Aw23000	86-09	MjesticVenture,DonRickls,GoGoRgl	6
5Aug84—Checked															

Aug 10 Sar 1 ft 1:412 b   ●Aug 3 Sar 6f ft 1:122 h   Jly 27 Sar 5f gd 1:02 h   Jly 20 Bel tr.t 6f ft 1:144 b

Majestic Venture

Own.—Hofmann Mrs P B — 115

B. c. 4, by Majestic Prince—Stick To Beauty, by Illustrious
Br.—Hofmann Mr-Mrs P B (Fla)
Tr.—Curtis William Jr
Lifetime 23 6 4 4 $117,323

1985	7	1	4	1	$46,987
1984	14	4	0	3	$63,616
Turf	2	0	0	0	

3Aug85-1Sar	7f	:22	:441	1:211ft	*8-5	115	31	32	47	511	Cruguet J6	Aw36000	85-11	KnghtfArmr,ThWddngGst,BBOfSts	7
16Jly85-5Mth	5f	:221	:45	:564ft	*1	120	21½	3½	33	24½	Rocco J3	Aw20000	97-17	DigginDitchs,MjstcVntur,M'ldy'sEgl	4
25Apr85-8GS	5f	:214	:442	:563ft	*3-2	117	53¼	31½	22½	22	CruguetJ4	Bld Rsng H	98-13	FortntProspct,MjstcVntr,ChfStwrd	8
25Apr85—Run in divisions; Hit gate															
14Apr85-8Aqu	6f	:222	:45	1:084ft	5	119	1hd	2½	35	37½	CruguetJ2	Bold Ruler	89-22	RockyMrrige,Entropy,MjesticVntur	6
14Apr85—Grade II															
27Mar85-9Hia	6f	:212	:443	1:09 ft	3-2	117	2½	21½	1hd	2nk	Cruguet J1	Kendall	96-17	FortntProspct,MjstcVntr,RxbryPrk	7
27Mar85—Steadied															
7Mar85-9Hia	6f	:22	:441	1:08 ft	*8-5	116	32	31	21	24	‡CrugutJ7	Tallahasse H	97-12	Erthmover,BirdisLgnd,MjsticVntur	8
‡7Mar85—Dead heat															
16Feb85-8GP	6f	:214	:441	1:091ft	8½	119	11½	13	15	11	Cruguet J4	Aw22200	93-21	MajesticVenture,DrnThtAlrm,Bello	6
8Sep84-7Bel	6f	:222	:452	1:093ft	6½	113	32½	21	22	32¼	Cruguet J6	Aw33000	92-17	RollinonOver,Thlssocrt,MjsticVntur	8

●Aug 12 Sar tr.t 3f ft :36 h   ●Jly 30 Sar 6f ft 1:122 h   Jly 23 Mth 3f ft :372 b   ●Jly 11 Mth 5f ft :584 hg

Faces Up

Own.—Tartan Stable — 115

B. g. 6, by What a Pleasure—Magic, by Buckpasser
Br.—Tartan Farms (Fla)
Tr.—Nerud Jan H
Lifetime 40 9 4 10 $198,400

1985	7	1	1	2	$30,180
1984	12	3	0	4	$67,900
Turf	2	0	0	0	

14Jun85-5Bel	7f	:231	:462	1:234ft	4	118	43	31½	1½	11¾	Cordero A Jr2	90000	83-24	Faces Up, Waitlist, Mr. Tatt	9
14Jun85—Slow st., clear															
31May85-5Bel	6½f	:223	:454	1:163ft	*1	112	53	41½	31	21½	Cordero A Jr7	75000	91-16	Red Medal, Faces Up, Talc Power	7
11May85-3Bel	6f	:221	:451	1:101ft	3	112	69	47	46	33	Cordero A Jr3	75000	88-12	MgneticFieldII,AgileShoebill,FcsUp	6
11May85—Off slowly															
19Apr85-7Aqu	7f	:223	:453	1:231sy	3½	117	44½	32½	33½	32¾	Cordero A Jr6	75000	82-22	Agile Shoebill, ShiningOut FacesUp	6
3Apr85-7Aqu	7f	:224	:444	1:204ft	9	119	79	79	611	513½	Vasquez J2	Aw36000	83-18	RockyMarriage,I'mSoMerry,Witlist	7
3Apr85—Slow early															
23Mar85-8Key	6f	:22	:452	1:101sy	6	114	63¾	612	612	610	Black AS2	Newtown H	80-25	Rocky Knave, Burts Star, Tarnish	6
11Mar85-8Aqu	6f	⊡:213	:44	1:091ft	7	119	611	610	69½	49½	Venezia M1	Aw36000	88-18	Mt.Livermore,AgileShoebill,Spendr	7
11Mar85—Began slowly															
31Dec84-5Med	6f	:23	:46	1:103ft	3¼	122	74½	54½	53½	31¾	Castaneda K1	Aw25000	87-22	Main Stem, Northern Ice, FacesUp	7

Jly 31 Sar 4f ft :49 b   Jly 24 Bel 4f ft :484 b   Jly 17 Bel 4f gd :59 b   Jly 11 Bel 4f ft :494 b

Copyright © 1985, by DAILY RACING FORM, INC.
Reprinted with permission of copyright owner.

Hamlet

Dk. b. or br. h. 5, by Key To The Kingdom—Saturday Matinee, by Silent Screen
Br.—Dimauro S A (NY) 1985 5 1 0 0 $9,000
Own.—Centennial Farms 115 Tr.—Connors Robert F 1984 7 3 0 0 $37,260
Lifetime 24 9 2 1 $93,546 Turf 3 1 0 0 $9,600

11Jly85-1GS 6f :22 :44^4 1:10^{4}ft 2½ 116 1½ 1^2 1^2 1¾ Vigliotti M J^7 40000 88-16 Hamlet, Top Knave, King's Bluff 7
18Jun85-8Mth 6f :22 :44^2 1:09^{1}ft 33 115 76½ 6^8 6^9 615¼ Vigliotti M J^4 Aw20000 79-14 VlintLrk,AmericnDibolo,Rumptious 7
18Jun85—Off slowly
8Jun85-8Mth 6f :22^4 :45^3 1:10 gd 9½ 115 12½ 13½ 1^2 55¼ Vigliotti M J^7 Aw20000 84-13 Rumptious,Now'sTheTime,RoccRel 7
25May85-7GS 5f :22 :44^4 :56^{3}ft 12 116 2^{hd} 2^{hd} 3^2 66¾ Vigliotti M J^2 Aw20000 93-12 Sagittarian,ChiefSteward,TitnRibot 6
12May85-8Del a5f Ⓣ:22^2 :46 :58^{1}fm 7 117 75¼ 8^8 10^9 109¼ VglttMJ^6 Post Card H 89-04 ‡RelibleJff,HrComsRd,LowllPrmir 10
3Sep84-9Del 5f Ⓣ:21^4 :44^2 :56^{1}fm*3-2 119 7^{11} 7^9 7^{14} 611¾ CastnedK^2 Postcard H 90-04 Jeff, Hawklike, Obgyn 7
5Aug84-7Sar 6f :22^1 :44^4 1:09^{3}ft 5 115 11½ 12½ 1½ 44¼ MacBeth D^3 Aw33000 88-09 Mugatea, All Fired Up, Sir Keys 6
26Jun84-9Mth 5f Ⓣ:23 :45^2 :57^{2}fm 4½ 122 1^{hd} 1^{hd} 1^1 1½ Castaneda K^8 Aw16000 96-04 Hamlet, Last of the Lot, FedFunds 8
●Aug 6 Sar 5f ft :58^4 h ●Jly 30 Del 4f ft :49 b Jly 20 Del 4f ft :49 b Jun 25 Del 4f ft :48^1 b

Cognizant

B. c. 4, by Explodent—I Understand, by Dr Fager
Br.—Happy Valley Farm &Peskoff (Fla) 1985 9 4 0 1 $36,770
Own.—Happy Valley Farm 108^7 Tr.—Dutrow Richard E 1984 5 M 0 0 $2,220
Lifetime 14 4 0 1 $38,990 Turf 2 0 0 0 $1,140

24Jly85-7Bel 7f :22^3 :45^1 1:22^{1}ft 5¼ 110^7 21½ 2^{hd} 11½ 15¼ Jones B S^1 Aw27000 91-17 Cognznt,MoonProspctor,SntorBrdy 7
15Jun85-6Bow 6f :23^1 :46^1 1:09^{4}ft 2 114^5 1½ 1^3 1^5 1^{11} Ramirez M R^2 Aw9500 91-20 Cognznt,ConslorJms,AlongCmJons 7
27May85-8Pim 6f :22^4 :45^1 1:10 ft 4 117^5 1½ 1^4 13½ 11¼ Jones S R^9 Aw11000 96-12 Cognizant, So Smart, Il Est Gran 10
20May85-7Pim 6f :22^4 :45^2 1:10^{3}ft *1 117^5 3^2 3^3 52½ 41¼ Jones S R^3 Aw11000 92-14 CountTheDots,IlEstGran,Asberhimi 6
1May85-6Pim 6f :23 :45^4 1:10 ft 6½ 117^5 32½ 3^{nk} 2^{hd} 1^{nk} Jones S R^9 Mdn 96-12 Cognizant, Sportive, Cyaneman 12
20Mar85-4Hia 1⅛ :48 1:12 1:51^{1}ft 10 122 1^{hd} 2^1 58½ 5^{11} Bailey J D^{12} Mdn 65-19 ‡ArcticSong,Nawannshar,Adorteur 12
13Mar85-6Hia 7f :23^1 :46 1:24^{1}ft 16 122 1^1 2^{hd} 2½ 3^3 Bailey J D^2 Mdn 79-18 Negev, Ahmad, Cognizant 10
22Feb85-3GP 1$\frac{1}{16}$:47 1:12^3 1:45^{3}ft 38 122 2^1 4^2 8^{14} 821¾ Bailey J D^2 Mdn 51-23 CommndrRb,ArctcSong,SothFlord 12
Aug 10 Sar 3f ft :36 b ●Aug 5 Sar 6f ft 1:12 h ●Jly 20 Aqu 5f ft :59^4 h Jly 15 Aqu 5f ft 1:00^3 h

Near The Storm

B. g. 3, by Near The High Sea—Stormy Haven, by Hasty Road
Br.—Fose Hill Farms (Ont-C) 1985 12 3 2 2 $52,444
Own.—Byers R 110 Tr.—McClachrie J D 1984 2 M 0 0
Lifetime 14 3 2 2 $52,444 Turf 2 0 0 0 $960

28Jly85-8WO 6f :21^3 :44^2 1:10 ft 5½ 117 2^1 1^{hd} 1^1 1¾ Fell J^7 HcpO 93-13 NrThStorm,P.J.Ruckus,ProudstHor 7
20Jly85-9WO 1 Ⓣ:46^{2}1:11^{1}1:37 fm 11 115 1^1 3^1 7^{11} 713¼ Dittfach H^2 Aw25000 79-12 Kzbek,CorncobsRoylty,ClssicRegnt 7
13Jly85-7WO 7f :22^4 :45^3 1:23^{3}ft *2½ 117 11½ 12½ 1^{hd} 33½ Dittfach H^7 Aw15000 87-19 Prkpsser,BishopsHill,NerTheStorm 8
30Jun85-6WO 7f Ⓣ:23^4 :46^{4}1:23^{2}fm 4¼ 114 3½ 32½ 41½ 4^2 Dittfach H^6 Aw16000 91-04 Blfrn,DevotedAllinc,Dnc'nForMony 6
15Jun85-10Tdn 1⅛ :46^2 1:11 1:49 sy 37 113 41½ 8^{13} 7^{19} 6^{21} DittfchH^2 Ohio Derby 71-15 SkipTrial,Encolure,JcqueL'Heureux 8
15Jun85—Grade II
30May85-8WO 7f :23 :46^1 1:24^{1}ft 2 116 1^{hd} 1^1 1^2 2^1 Dittfach H^4 ⓈAw15000 87-24 HonordConsl,NrThStorm,MstrLrnz 7
19May85-9WO 7f :22^3 :45 1:24 ft 4¾ 115 14½ 1^3 21½ 3^2 Fell J^4 ⓈQueenston 87-22 RglSnow,PrEmptivStrk,NrThStorm 7
19May85—Grade III-C
8May85-8WO 6f :22^4 :45^2 1:10^{4}ft *3-2 116 11½ 14½ 1^6 15½ Fell J^6 Aw14500 89-21 NrThStorm,StolThPrinc,JmmdGold 8
Aug 11 WO tr.t 3f gd :36^4 h ●Jly 11 WO 3f ft :35^2 b Jun 28 WO Ⓣ 3f fm :34^2 h

Mayanesian

Ch. h. 6, by Bold Hour—Cozumel, by T V Lark
Br.—Madden Preston (Ky) 1985 10 1 1 0 $27,440
Own.—Gordonsdale Farm 117 Tr.—Zito Nicholas P 1984 12 2 3 0 $68,195
Lifetime 64 9 10 5 $253,057 Turf 11 2 4 1 $93,060

19Jly85-7Bel 6f Ⓣ:21^2 :44^{2}1:09^{4}fm 2¾ 122 31½ 33½ 32½ 21¼ Cordero AJr^6 Aw36000 90-14 ZanyTactics,Maynesin,RiverDemon 6
6Jly85-7Mth 5f :22^2 :45^3 :57^{4}ft 6½ 115 3^{nk} 4¾ 3^1 11¼ Cordero A Jr^5 HcpO 97-17 Maynesin,ShrpLittleGirl,RelibleJeff 7
30Jun85-7Bel 6f Ⓣ:21^4 :44^{3}1:09^{2}fm 9¼ 117 21½ 43½ 5^5 45¼ Ward W A^5 Aw36000 88-18 Alev, Equalize, River Demon 6
15Jun85-7Bel 1$\frac{1}{16}$ Ⓣ:45^{2}1:09^{2}1:41 fm 11 117 74½ 7^7 6^8 67¾ Ward W A^1 Aw40000 83-18 Fortnightly,HighIce,FearlessLeder 10
6Jun85-8Bel 6f :22^1 :44^4 1:10^{2}gd 10 113 3^3 3^5 65½ 63¼ Ward W A^1 HcpO 87-15 Basket Weave, River Demon, Alev 7
10May85-8Bel 6f :22^1 :45^2 1:11 ft 8 114^{10} 7^{11} 7^{16} 7^{16} 716¼ Falcone J^5 Aw36000 71-20 Cozzene, Basket Weave,MomentoII 7
25Apr85-6GS 5f :22 :44^1 :56^{1}ft 8½ 115 3^1 54¾ 48½ 59½ WrdWA^3 Bld ResongH 92-13 Rollin on Over, Roast, Burts Star 6
25Apr85—Run in divisions
17Mar85-9Hia 6f :21^2 :44^3 1:09 ft 21 119 1½ 11½ 45½ 610¾ Bailey J D^7 Kendall 85-17 FortntProspct,MjstcVntr,RxbryPrk 7
Aug 10 Sar 4f ft :47 h Aug 3 Sar 3f ft :34^1 h Jly 28 Sar tr.t 4f ft :49^4 b Jly 15 Bel 4f ft :47^2 h

Copyright © 1985, by DAILY RACING FORM, INC.
Reprinted with permission of copyright owner.

and won that race, winning $15,000, while in 1984, he ran 3 times and won twice, winning $22,800.

Now, examining the past performance chart of Loud and Clear, we see that his last race was on August 5, 1985, ten days before, and he raced at Saratoga in the seventh race, and the race was at 6 furlongs. The fractional times of the race were :22⁴ (at 2 furlongs), 45³ (at 4 furlongs) and 1:10¹ (at 6 furlongs) on a fast (ft) track.

The winning time at the race was 1:10¹ and the fractional times prior to the winning time were set by the horse leading at that distance. Thus, after 2 furlongs, the horse in the lead ran it in 22⁴, while at 4 furlongs the pace was 45³. All fractional times in horseracing are to fifths, thus the times were listed as 22 and 4/5 seconds, 45 and 3/5 seconds and the final time was 1 minute ten and 1/5 seconds.

Next we see the number 2½, which signifies the odds that Loud and Clear went off at, which was 2½-1 or 5-2. He carried 117 pounds in that race, and his *calls* (position in the field) were second, first, first and first, winning the race by one and 3/4 lengths, after first leading by a head, then two lengths and then finishing well ahead of the second horse, which was Silver Slate.

There were 7 horses in this race, and it was an allowance race worth $25,000. Loud and Clear's *speed rating* was 89-16, which means that compared to the track record, which would be 100, Loud and Clear ran an 89. This is a good effort. The 16 *variant*, means that the average horse was 16 points off the 100 mark that day, and since the track was fast, it meant that the horses were rated for speed at an average 84, and so Loud and Clear was five points above that average.

The track variant can mean either the quality of the horses running that day, the condition of the track, or both. Speed ratings are important when a group of horses have run at the same track. The quality of horses at Saratoga will be better than those at a lesser-known track, and a horse with a 95 speed rating at Woodbine, for example, wouldn't compare favorably with a 90 rating at a top track like Belmont.

Thus, speed ratings must be examined in perspective. They will have validity only when at comparable tracks. In New York, for example, the speed ratings at Belmont, Aqueduct and Saratoga will be fairly comparable. All are punishing tracks with deep soil, not the cardboard fast tracks favored in the West. Plus the caliber of the horses running at these tracks is very high. They get the best.

An examination of Loud and Clear's races shows that he ran in a Maiden Race at Belmont on September 29, 1983, going off at 41-1 and finishing second. Thereafter, after this first effort, he was in three other maiden races, and finally he *broke his maiden* on August 10, 1984 at Saratoga, winning by 5-3/4 lengths.

He's been run sparsely, only having six races in the last two years, but he's won his last three races convincingly. However, he's going from an allowance race worth $25,000 to one worth $36,000. Thus, as the horse players say, the colt is *moving up in class.*

In this same race, there are other horses which have won considerably more money than Loud and Clear, whose lifetime earnings are $44,600. This figure is seen just below the trainer's name, and just above the last race he ran on August 5th, 1985.

The horse with the most lifetime winnings is Mayanesian, who has garnered $253,057. Next comes Faces Up with $198,400 and then The Wedding Guest, with $194,386. The Wedding Guest, however, is a four-year-old colt, while the two others are six years old. Mayanesian is a **horse**, the term used for a male five years or older, while Faces Up is a **gelding**, which means it has been gelded, the term used by horsemen for castration, and thus Faces Up is **unsexed**. Male horses are occasionally gelded as the only way to control and train them correctly for running. Some of the greatest horses in the history of racing, such as Kelso and John Henry, have been geldings. Indeed, the greatest money winner of all time was John Henry, and Kelso isn't far behind.

Geldings of high quality often win enormous sums of money for their owners because they're allowed to race into their 9th and 10th years, since they can't be retired for stud purposes.

More important than overall lifetime winnings would be the record of winnings for the last two years. In this regard, The Wedding Guest has done best of the horses in this race. He won $162,666 in 1984, winning four of ten starts, placing one time and coming in third, or showing, once.

However, we find that his 1985 winnings of

$31,320 is not the best of all the horses running. The 1985 winning record belongs to River Demon. This four-year-old colt has been in the money seven of nine times, winning three of those races. He has gradually moved up from $18,000 to $36,000 allowance races, and finished third three times in a row, racing for that money.

In this section, we're not handicapping the race, just showing the number of factors that can be considered from reading the past performance charts. They tell us all we have to know about the past seven or eight races each horse has run, but the race we have to bet on will reveal the present condition of each horse. However, by that time we've made our bets and it's too late to recant. So, we turn to another bit of information shown in these charts that may help us to know the horse's present condition, and that is the workout times. These are listed at the bottom of each horse's charts.

These are important to us only after the last posted race. Loud and Clear has had two workouts, both times on the track at Saratoga. He did 3 furlongs in 39, **breezing** (:39b) and 5 furlongs in 1:04, also breezing, both times on fast tracks.

Breezing is slower than **handily**, or in hand, signified by an "h" next to the time of the workout. These terms signify a pace much slower than that used in an actual race. Cognizant, who hasn't run since July 24th, 1985, has two workouts listed since then, one of 3 furlongs on a fast Saratoga track in :36 breezing, and once on August 5th, on the same fast track, doing 6 furlongs in 1:12 handily. Cognizant has won his last three races, his last two very easily, but he hasn't run at Saratoga yet this year.

As we go along explaining all the information available, we can see how many variables have to be studied for each race, and this is what makes handicapping so fascinating and difficult at the same time.

One final note: we discussed the speed rating and track variant briefly in this section, but these are important factors in handicapping races, and the following is a detailed explanation of just how these two figures are arrived at.

Speed Ratings

A **speed rating** compares the horse's final time to the track record at that distance established in a prior season. This track record has a rating of 100. Since a difference of length (horse's length) is approximately 1/5 of a second, for each 1/5 of a second that the horse is slower than the track record, one point is deducted.

Thus, if a horse is two seconds off the track record (10 lengths behind) he would receive a speed rating of 90. Should a horse be 10 lengths behind the winning horse in a race, in which the winner was one second slower than the track record, then that losing horse's speed rating would only be 85. For example, if the track record for 6 furlongs was 1:09, and the winner ran the race in 1:10, then the horse 10 lengths behind would have a time of approximately 1:12 and the 85 speed rating.

Track Variants

Next to the speed rating is another number, called the **track variant**. For example, if the speed rating is 85 for a horse, you might see 85-18. The second number, 18, is the track variant.

This is calculated by taking into consideration all of the races run by horses on that particular day, their quality, the condition of the track, or a combination of both. All the speed ratings of winners are added up, then an average is taken dividing that number by the races run that day. For example, if the average speed rating came to 82 for winning horses, then that number is subtracted from 100, giving us a track variant for that day of 18, the difference between 100 and 82. The lower the track variant, the faster the track that day, or the better was the quality of the horses running.

VI. Explanation of Abreviations Used in Racing Charts

There are a number of abbreviations that should be known by horseplayers in order to better understand the information presented in racing charts. The following are the ones most frequently encountered.

Types of Race.

The *Daily Racing Form* designates a claiming race simply by showing a money amount without any other notation.

Chart 6
Types of Races

15000—This would indicate a claiming race in which this horse could be claimed for $15,000. If the horse had been claimed in that race, the notation would read: **c15000**.

M15000—Maiden Claiming Race.

15000H—Claiming Handicap Race.

Other race categories are as follows:

Mdn—Maiden Race, in which none of the horses have won a race previously.

AlwM—Maiden Allowance Race for non-winners with special weight allowances.

Aw36000—An Allowance Race, showing the purse value of the race.

Hcp—Handicap Race. When the reading is **HcpO**, it means an overnight handicap race.

Stakes Races—In a Stakes Race, the name of the race is listed, or an abbreviation of that name. When you see just a name listed, such as Preakness or Gold Cup, you know that this is a stakes race. When there's an H next to the stakes name, such as Bing CrosbyH at Del Mar, then it's a stakes handicap race.

Track Conditions

In the past performance charts, the condition of the track is listed next to the time of the race. For example, if the final time in a 6 furlong race is listed as $1:11^2$ft, then we know the track was fast for that time. If it had been listed as $1:11^2$gd, the time for that race was run by a horse on a good track.

It's important to know the symbols for track conditions because some horses prefer mud and slop and others will only do their best on a fast track. If a horse has an off race it may be due solely to track conditions.

Chart 7
Track Conditions

Ft—Fast track. The track is dry and hard.

Gd—Good track. The track is not quite dry.

Sl—Slow track. The track is wet and drying out, but not good.

Sly—Sloppy track. The track is firm with puddles of water on its surface.

My—Muddy track. The track is soft from top to bottom.

Hy—Heavy track. The track features the slowest of all conditions.

Finishing Results

The order of the horse's finish is signified by a number. If the horse came in first, it would be a 1. After the number is the winning margin. The narrowest of margins is a nose, then comes a head, then a neck. These are listed as follows in the past performance and official racing charts:

no—nose
hd—head
nk—neck

The following would show a horse's running of a race, with position and margins. If a horse is not in the lead, then the number after his position would indicate how many lengths he's behind the leader.

6^3 $4^{2\frac{1}{2}}$ 3^{nk} 2^{hd} 1no $1^{1\frac{1}{2}}$

The horse was first sixth, three lengths behind the leader, then he improved his position to fourth, 2½ lengths behind the first horse, then he was third by a neck, then second by a head, then took the lead by a nose, then won the race by 1½ lengths.

Workouts

In order for bettors to get a better indication of the condition of a horse, especially one that hasn't raced for a while, he or she can examine the workouts of the horse. These are listed under the past performances for each horse, showing the date, the time of the workout, and how the horse was handled.

Let's look at a sample workout to see what all this means.

Aug 23 Sar 5f gd 1:01 h

The horse had a workout on August 23rd at Saratoga, the distance was 5 furlongs on a good track, and the time was one minute and one second, and the horse ran handily.

In workouts, horses aren't usually pushed to the limit the way they are in a race, and so the workout times are generally much slower than the actual time the horse could run the race. Also horses don't usually break from a gate, and simply run from one furlong pole to another, and are timed for that distance. The following are abbreviations commonly used in workouts:

Chart 8
Workout Paces

b—breezing	
e—easily	**d—driving**
h—handily	**g—worked from gate**

Workout times are often deceptive because the horses aren't working from a gate and aren't in competition with other horses and are not running at full speed, but sometimes it's a good indication of the condition of the horse, especially if you see the letter "d" indicating that the horse was driving, going all out.

Sex of Horse

There are six categories listed under sex.

Chart 9
Abbreviations Used for Sex of Horse

c—Colt. This is a male horse under the age of 5 years.

f—Filly. This is a female under the age of 5 years.

h—Horse. This is a male 5 years or older.

m—Mare. This is a female five years or older.

g—Gelding. This is an unsexed or gelded male of any age.

rig—Ridgling. This is a horse with undescended testicles (half-castrated) of any age.

Color

Horses come in a variety of colors, ranging from black to white, with browns predominating.

Chart 10
Abbreviations Used for Color of Horse

Ch—Chestnut	B—Bay.
Gr—Gray	Blk—Black.
Ro—Roan	Br—Brown
Wh—White	

Dk—Dark, as in Dk b or Dk br, which would mean dark bay or dark brown.

VII. Understanding Official Racing Charts

The Official Racing Charts show the results of each race run, so that not only do we know the order of finish of all the horses, but observations are made about each horse's running. The serious bettor would do well to save these results, and examine them. They, together with the past performance charts, give a very clear picture of just how each horse did in a particular race.

Let's examine several of the official racing charts for Monday, August 12, 1985 at Saratoga.

The first race was 1-1/16 miles on the *inner turf*. Normally races are held on the dirt track, and unless otherwise marked in the program or chart, it is assumed the race took place on dirt. The dirt tracks in New York are much deeper than those in California, and therefore faster times are recorded in California, won by mediocre horses. **Turf races** are held on grass.

Chart 11

Official Racing Charts—Saratoga, 8/12/85

OWNERS, TRAINERS LISTED IN ORDER OF HORSES' ORIGINAL FINISH POSITION.

FIRST RACE
Saratoga
AUGUST 12, 1985

1 1/16 MILES.(InnerTurf). (1.41) CLAIMING. Purse $26,000. Fillies and mares. 3-years-old and upward. Weight: 3-year-olds 117 lbs. Older 122 lbs. Non-winners of two races at a mile or over since July 1 allowed 3 lbs. Of such a race since then 5 lbs. Claiming price $75,000 for each $2,500 to $70,000, 2 lbs. (Races when entered to be claimed for $65,000 or less not considered). (12th Day. WEATHER CLEAR. TEMPERATURE 73 DEGREES).

Value of race $26,000; value to winner $15,600; second $5,720; third $3,120; fourth $1,560. Mutuel pool $104,965, OTB pool $139,959.

Last Raced	Horse	Eqt.	A.	Wt	PP	St	¼	½	¾	Str	Fin	Jockey	Cl'g Pr	Odds $1
19Jly85 ^{4}Bel^{5}	Marked Lady	b	4	113	9	8	5^{2}	4^{1}	$2^{\frac{1}{2}}$	$1^{\frac{1}{2}}$	1^{hd}	Santagata N	70000	b-5.90
31Jly85 ^{6}Sar^{4}	Tricky Tune	b	4	117	3	2	4^{hd}	5^{2}	$6^{\frac{1}{2}}$	2^{1}	$2^{2\frac{1}{2}}$	Vasquez J	75000	6.30
4Aug85 ^{4}Sar^{1}	Dawna	b	6	113	6	6	$3^{1\frac{1}{2}}$	3^{hd}	$3^{\frac{1}{2}}$	$4^{2\frac{1}{2}}$	$3^{1\frac{1}{2}}$	Cruguet J	70000	2.20
5Aug85 ^{4}Sar^{5}	Silver Bluff Road		5	113	1	9	9	$7^{1\frac{1}{2}}$	$8^{1\frac{1}{2}}$	$5^{\frac{1}{2}}$	4^{nk}	Samyn J L	70000	23.00
18Jly85 ^{7}Bel^{7}	Free Saint	b	7	113	7	5	$1^{1\frac{1}{2}}$	$1^{1\frac{1}{2}}$	1^{1}	$3^{\frac{1}{2}}$	5^{2}	Cordero A Jr	70000	b-5.90
1Jly85 ^{6}AP^{2}	Sea Shell		6	113	8	4	2^{hd}	2^{hd}	$4^{1\frac{1}{2}}$	6^{1}	6^{1}	Day P	70000	6.10
5Aug85 ^{2}Sar^{4}	Maidenhead	b	6	115	2	1	$8^{\frac{1}{2}}$	9	9	$8^{1\frac{1}{2}}$	7^{hd}	MacBeth D	72500	2.70
26Jly85 ^{9}Mth^{6}	Temple Goddess		4	113	4	3	$6^{\frac{1}{2}}$	8^{2}	$7^{\frac{1}{2}}$	$7^{1\frac{1}{2}}$	$8^{4\frac{1}{4}}$	Velasquez J	70000	9.10
4Aug85 ^{4}Sar^{2}	Areobics	b	4	113	5	7	7^{1}	6^{hd}	5^{hd}	9	9	Lovato F Jr	70000	12.30

b-Coupled: Marked Lady and Free Saint.

OFF AT 1:30. Start good, Won driving. Time, :23⅘, :48, 1:12⅖, 1:37⅘, 1:44⅖ Course firm.

Official Program Numbers↘

$2 Mutuel Prices:	**2-(J)-MARKED LADY (b-entry)**	**13.80**	**6.60**	**3.80**
	5-(C)-TRICKY TUNE		**7.60**	**3.80**
	1-(G)-DAWNA			**2.80**

B. f, by Singh—Miss Marked, by Raise A Cup. Trainer Schaeffer Stephen. Bred by Triggs D & J (Fla).

MARKED LADY, never far back, rallied to catch FREE SAINT leaving the far turn and lasted over TRICKY TUNE in a long drive. The latter made a run along the inside after entering the stretch but wasn't good enough in a stiff drive. DAWNA, well placed to the stretch, came out for the drive but lacked the needed rally. SILVER BLUFF ROAD failed to seriously menace. FREE SAINT was used up making the pace. SEA SHELL gave way leaving the far turn. MAIDENHEAD was always outrun. TEMPLE GODDESS raced wide. AREOBICS moved within striking distance midway of the far turn but lacked a further response.

Owners— 1, Spiegel R; 2, Bourbon Hills Farm; 3, Davis A; 4, Dunn D Joy; 5, Spiegel R; 6, Aitken L F; 7, Gagliano S; 8, Epstein Mrs Adele; 9, Keller M.

Trainers— 1, Schaeffer Stephen; 2, Trovato Joseph A; 3, Moschera Gasper S; 4, Koller Peggy; 5, Schaeffer Stephen; 6, Vanier Harvey L; 7, Barrera Oscar S; 8, Skiffington Thomas; 9, Ribaudo Robert.

Scratched—Brutish Beast (12Jly85 ^{4}Bel^{8}); Outofthequestion (4Aug85 ^{4}Sar^{3}).

SECOND RACE
Saratoga
AUGUST 12, 1985

1 ⅛ MILES. (1.47) CLAIMING. Purse $18,000. 3-year-olds and upward. Weight: 3-year-olds 117 lbs. Older 122 lbs. Non-winners of two races at a mile or over since July 1 allowed 3 lbs. Of such a race since then 5 lbs. Claiming price $25,000; for each $2,500 to $20,000, 2 lbs. (Races when entered to be claimed for $18,000 or less not considered).

Value of race $18,000; value to winner $10,800; second $3,960; third $2,160; fourth $1,080. Mutuel pool $101,859, OTB pool $102,892. Quinella Pool $124,050. OTB Quinella Pool $170,582.

Last Raced	Horse	Eqt.	A.	Wt	PP	St	¼	½	¾	Str	Fin	Jockey	Cl'g Pr	Odds $1
29Jly85 ^{4}Bel^{7}	Lead The Way	b	5	115	2	1	$2^{1\frac{1}{2}}$	2^{hd}	$2^{1\frac{1}{2}}$	2^{2}	1^{hd}	Maple E	22500	6.70
24Jly85 ^{10}Mth^{1}	Rainbow Castle	b	4	110	7	2	1^{1}	$1^{\frac{1}{2}}$	$1^{\frac{1}{2}}$	1^{hd}	2^{2}	Alvarez A†^{5}	22500	3.60
8Aug85 ^{9}Sar^{2}	Bambolino	b	6	115	1	4	$4^{1\frac{1}{2}}$	$4^{1\frac{1}{2}}$	$3^{1\frac{1}{2}}$	3^{3}	3^{3}	Lovato F Jr	22500	1.90
1Aug85 ^{2}Sar^{5}	Feeling Too Much		6	117	6	7	$7^{\frac{1}{2}}$	6^{1}	$5^{\frac{1}{2}}$	$4^{\frac{1}{2}}$	4^{2}	Davis R G	25000	7.60
1Aug85 ^{2}Sar^{4}	What Nonsense		5	106	5	5	3^{1}	3^{2}	4^{3}	$5^{1\frac{1}{2}}$	5^{hd}	Verro N^{7}	20000	27.50
31Jly85 ^{4}Sar^{8}	Limbo	b	3	105	8	6	8	8	7^{3}	7^{10}	6^{nk}	Decarlo C P^{7}	25000	17.30
9Aug85 ^{9}Sar^{5}	Charmed Rook	b	4	119	3	3	5^{1}	5^{4}	6^{4}	6^{hd}	7^{15}	Vasquez J	25000	2.40
10Jly85 ^{2}Bel^{6}	Abri Fiscal	b	4	103	4	8	6^{3}	7^{2}	8	8	8	Carter T^{10}	20000	35.20

OFF AT 2:01 Start good, Won driving. Time, :24, :48, 1:12⅗, 1:38⅗, 1:51⅘ Track fast.

$2 Mutuel Prices:	**2-(B)-LEAD THE WAY**	**15.40**	**6.80**	**3.80**
	8-(I)-RAINBOW CASTLE		**5.00**	**3.20**
	1-(A)-BAMBOLINO			**2.80**
	$2 QUINELLA 2-8 PAID $40.80.			

Ch. g, by Mr Leader—Couldn't Be Better, by Better Bee. Trainer Brennan Pat. Bred by Smith Sarah Louise (Va).

LEAD THE WAY, prominent from the outset, drifted out slightly leaving the far turn, then continued on gamely to wear down RAINBOW CASTLE in the final yards. The latter saved ground while making the pace, held a narrow lead into the stretch and fought it out willingly. BAMBOLINO came out while rallying approaching the stretch but lacked the needed late response. FEELING TOO MUCH finished evenly. WHAT NONSENSE made a run from the outside midway along the backstretch but was finished on the far turn. CHARED ROOK had no apparent excuse. ABRI FISCA broke slowly.

Owners— 1, Otis Constance; 2, Lane Glenn; 3, Martin Glorida; 4, A Davis; 5, Springhill Stable; 6, Judd Monte Farm; 7, Kogstat H G; 8, Gampel H A.

Trainers— 1, Brennan Pat; 2, Sedlacek Michael C; 3, Martin Jose; 4, Moschera Gasper S; 5, Paus A; 6, Maxwell Adrian J; 7, Lake Robert P; 8, Gullo Thomas J.

† **Apprentice allowance waived:** Rainbow Castle 2 pounds.

Scratched—Deedee's Deal (5Aug85 ^{1}Sar^{5}); Sidi Bou Said (5Aug85 ^{9}Sar^{8}).

$2 Daily Double 2-2 Paid $133.80. Daily Double Pool $281,450. OTB Daily Double Pool $439,015.

Copyright © 1985, by DAILY RACING FORM, INC.
Reprinted with permission of copyright owner.

THIRD RACE

Saratoga

AUGUST 12, 1985

7 FURLONGS. (1.20$\frac{3}{5}$) CLAIMING. Purse $20,000. Fillies, 3-year-olds. Weight, 121 lbs. Non-winners of two races since July 1 allowed 3 lbs. Of a race since the, 5 lbs. Claiming price $50,000 for each $2,500 to $45,000 allowed 2 lbs. (Races when entered to be claimed for $40,000 or less not considered.)

Value of race $20,000; value to winner $12,000; second $4,400; third $2,400; fourth $1,200. Mutuel pool $132,156, OTB pool $101,456. Exacta Pool $181,022. OTB Exacta Pool $204,736.

Last Raced	Horse	Eqt.	A.	Wt	PP	St	¼	½	Str	Fin	Jockey	Cl'g Pr	Odds $1
27Jly85 ^{1}Bel^{1}	A Hot Number	b	3	111	7	2	5^{2}	3^{3}	1^{hd}	1^{3}	Decarlo C P^{7}	50000	5.00
7Aug85 ^{1}Sar^{7}	Sherry B.	b	3	109	6	4	$1^{1\frac{1}{2}}$	1^{3}	$2^{2\frac{1}{2}}$	$2^{1\frac{1}{2}}$	Privitera R^{5}	45000	1.00
20Jly85 ^{1}Bel^{7}	Bare Assets	b	3	105	2	8	8	7^{3}	3^{4}	$3^{2\frac{3}{4}}$	Jones B S^{5}	45000	13.60
27Jly85 ^{1}Bel^{6}	Right Girl	b	3	112	3	7	7^{1}	6^{hd}	5^{1}	4no	Velasquez J	45000	17.00
12Jly85 ^{2}Bel^{1}	Inherently		3	107	5	5	$2^{1\frac{1}{2}}$	$2^{\frac{1}{2}}$	4^{hd}	$5^{2\frac{1}{2}}$	Wynter N A^{7}	47500	8.40
2Aug85 ^{1}Sar^{6}	Same Sweet You	b	3	112	4	6	$4^{1\frac{1}{2}}$	$4^{1\frac{1}{2}}$	6^{8}	$6^{10\frac{1}{2}}$	Day P	45000	8.10
17Jly85 ^{7}Bel^{6}	Sham's Beauty		3	116	8	3	3^{hd}	5^{2}	$7^{1\frac{1}{2}}$	7^{2}	Santos J A	50000	44.20
8Aug85 ^{1}Sar^{6}	Boris The Cat	b	3	112	9	1	6^{4}	8	8	8	MacBeth D	45000	7.10
2Aug85 ^{2}Sar^{10}	Memorable Melody	b	3	116	1	—	—	—	—	–	Graell A	50000	12.70

Memorable Melody, Lost rider.

OFF AT 2:33 Start good for all but MEMORABLE MELODY, Won ridden out. Time, :23, :46$\frac{3}{5}$, 1:11$\frac{1}{5}$, 1:25 Track fast.

$2 Mutuel Prices:				
	7-(G)-A HOT NUMBER	12.00	4.00	3.00
	6-(F)-SHERRY B.		3.20	2.60
	2-(B)-BARE ASSETS			4.20

$2 EXACTA 7-6 PAID $30.20.

Ch. f, by Spellcaster—Princess Rain, by Rainy Lake. Trainer Sedlacek Sue. Bred by Appleton A I (Fla).

A HOT NUMBER moved through along the inside midway of the turn, came out to continue her rally, caught SHERRY B. near the final furlong and drew away. The latter made the pace into the stretch while racing slightly out from the rail but was no match for the winner. BARE ASSETS rallied along the inside near midstretch but failed to sustain her bid. RIGHT GIRL failed to be a serious factor. INHERENTLY tired. SAME SWEET YOU was finished early. SHAM'S BEAUTY tired badly while racing wide. BORIS THE CAT was always outrun. MEMORABLE MELODY stumbled badly following the start unseating her rider.

Owners— 1, Tresvant Stable; 2, Barrera O S; 3, Kimmel C P; 4, Garren M M; 5, Harbor View Farm; 6, Godshall Joanne; 7, Simon M; 8, Levien A N; 9, Live Oak Plantation.

Trainers— 1, Sedlacek Sue; 2, Barrera Oscar S; 3, Toner James J; 4, Garren Murray M; 5, Martin Frank; 6, Godshall Joanne; 7, Campo John P; 8, Pascuma Warren J; 9, Kelly Patrick J.

Corrected weight: Bare Assets 105 pounds.

FOURTH RACE

Saratoga

AUGUST 12, 1985

1 $\frac{1}{16}$ MILES.(InnerTurf). (1.41) CLAIMING. Purse $23,000. 3-year-olds and upward. Weight: 3-year-olds 117 lbs. Older 122 lbs. Non-winners of two races at a mile or over since July 1 allowed 3 lbs. Of such a race since then 5 lbs. Claiming price $50,000; for each $2,500 to $45,000, 2 lbs. (Races when entered to be claimed for $40,000 or less not considered).

Value of race $23,000; value to winner $13,800; second $5,060; third $2,760; fourth $1,380. Mutuel pool $165,828, OTB pool $114,464. Q Pl $84,682.OTB Pl $102,072.Ex Pl $117,759. OTB Pl $134,214

Last Raced	Horse	Eqt.	A.	Wt	PP	St	¼	½	¾	Str	Fin	Jockey	Cl'g Pr	Odds $1
31Jly85 ^{4}Sar^{6}	Ski Fleet	b	4	113	9	8	$8^{2\frac{1}{2}}$	9^{10}	7^{5}	$4^{1\frac{1}{2}}$	$1^{\frac{1}{2}}$	Cordero A Jr	45000	7.50
28Jly85 ^{7}WO^{5}	Rocamadour II		6	117	7	10	9^{5}	$8^{\frac{1}{2}}$	$4^{\frac{1}{2}}$	$1^{\frac{1}{2}}$	$2^{2\frac{1}{4}}$	Maple E	50000	2.30
17Jly85 ^{2}Bel^{2}	Greyfield		4	113	3	4	6^{5}	6^{3}	$5^{1\frac{1}{2}}$	2^{hd}	$3^{1\frac{1}{2}}$	Hernandez R	45000	12.30
3Aug85 ^{7}Sar^{7}	Dominating Dooley	b	5	117	2	1	$2^{\frac{1}{2}}$	$2^{1\frac{1}{2}}$	2^{2}	3^{1}	$4^{1\frac{1}{2}}$	Cruguet J	50000	1.70
17Jly85 ^{2}Bel^{1}	Saratoga Reverie		5	115	5	7	7^{2}	$7^{\frac{1}{2}}$	6^{hd}	7^{4}	$5^{1\frac{1}{2}}$	Davis R G	45000	11.30
24Jly85 ^{7}WO^{7}	Misty Vow		4	113	1	2	4^{hd}	$3^{\frac{1}{2}}$	$3^{1\frac{1}{2}}$	6^{1}	$6^{\frac{1}{2}}$	Samyn J L	45000	12.40
17Jly85 ^{2}Bel^{3}	Equity Kicker		4	113	8	9	10	10	9^{hd}	8^{6}	7^{3}	Velasquez J	45000	15.80
17Jly85 ^{2}Bel^{6}	Trinbago Pride	b	4	106	6	3	1^{1}	1^{hd}	1^{hd}	5^{hd}	$8^{3\frac{1}{2}}$	Jones B S^{7}	45000	37.40
20Jly85 ^{4}Bel^{1}	Individual Lad		5	108	10	6	5^{2}	4^{hd}	$8^{\frac{1}{2}}$	9^{2}	$9^{10\frac{1}{2}}$	Alvarez A†^{5}	45000	10.30
20Jly85 ^{4}Bel^{7}	El Fantasma	b	7	113	4	5	$3^{\frac{1}{2}}$	5^{1}	10	10	10	Santagata N	45000	39.50

OFF AT 3:06 Start good, Won driving. Time, :22$\frac{4}{5}$, :47, 1:11, 1:36$\frac{2}{5}$, 1:43 Course firm.

$2 Mutuel Prices:				
	9-(I)-SKI FLEET	17.00	6.40	4.40
	7-(G)-ROCAMADOUR II		4.80	3.40
	3-(C)-GREYFIELD			7.40

$2 QUINELLA 7-9 PAID $37.00. $2 EXACTA 9-7 PAID $90.40.

Gr. c, by Alias Smith—Gloriosky, by Alcibiades II. Trainer Gullo Gary. Bred by Roth E (Md).

SKI FLEET, outrun early, made a run along the inside after entering the stretch and outfinished ROCAMADOUR II. The latter moved boldly from the outside to reach the front nearing the final furlong but wasn't able to withstand the winner. GREYFIELD made a bold bid along the inside after entering the stretch but weakened under pressure. DOMINATING DOOLEY went up after TRINBAGO PRIDE on the backstretch, dueled for the lead to midstretch and gave way. SARATOGA REVERIE failed to be a serious factor. MISTY VOW tired. TRINBAGO PRIDE was used up vying for the lead. INDIVIDUAL LAD tired badly. EL FANTASMA was finished soon after going a half.

Owners— 1, Costello W B Jr; 2, Buckley R J; 3, Douglass R F; 4, Davis A; 5, Happy Valley Farm; 6, Knob Hill Stable; 7, Hellson Stable; 8, Tatt Stables; 9, C'est Tout Stable; 10, Singin Frog Stable.

Trainers— 1, Gullo Gary; 2, Doyle Mike J; 3, Nesky Kenneth A; 4, Moschera Gasper S; 5, Barrera Luis; 6, Vella Daniel J; 7, Hertler John O; 8, Widmer Wayne; 9, Lake Robert P; 10, Alvarez Louis C.

† **Apprentice allowance waived:** Individual Lad 2 pounds.

Rocamadour II was claimed by Twin Bee Stable; trainer, LaBoccetta Frank.

Scratched—Hueco (14Jly85 ^{3}Bel^{8}); Century Banker (27Jly85 ^{8}Rkm^{5}); Bold Bob's Dusty (10Aug85 ^{9}Sar^{8}); Cantonero (31Jly85 ^{4}Sar^{7}); Nawannshar (31Jly85 ^{4}Sar^{5}); Clarinet King (31Jly85 ^{4}Sar^{2}); Cathedral Bells (7Jly85 ^{2}Bel^{7}); All Night Stand (5Aug85 ^{1}Sar^{3}).

Copyright © 1985, by DAILY RACING FORM, INC.
Reprinted with permission of copyright owner.

This first race was for a purse of $26,000 and was a claiming race. Claiming races are the cheapest of all races and generally attract the weaker horses. They're called claiming races because, as we mentioned before, any of the horses running can be claimed by another owner or stable that is racing at that track.

Better horses, or horses with potential, will be run in other than claiming races, for the owners of these quality horses don't want to risk losing their horses to another owner through a claim. In this first race, the claiming price is unusually high, running from $70,000 to $75,000. In cheaper claiming races at minor racetracks, horses can be claimed for as little as $1,000 and in some instances, for even less.

But Saratoga is a quality track, and the horses in this race are **fillies** and **mares**, three years old and upward. A filly becomes a mare at the age of five. If we continue to read the fine print above the chart, we see the conditions of the race as far as weight and claiming price go. Also the purses are shown. Out of a $26,000 total purse, the winner gets $15,600, which is 60% of the entire purse. The horse placing, or finishing second, gets $5,720, and the show horse receives $3,120, with the horse finishing fourth getting $1,560, or 1/10th the money the winner receives. There is no purse for any horse running worse than fourth.

In New York tracks, there is not only a mutuel pool comprising all the bets at the track, but an OTB (Off Track Betting) pool, showing all the money bet away from the racetrack.

The winner was Marked Lady, who ran from post position 9. Marked Lady was coupled with Free Saint in the betting, and thus the bettor got two horses for the price of one. Although Marked Lady ran from the 9th position, its number was 2 in the betting at the track, and (J) at the OTB offices. We see this by looking at the payoff next to $2 Mutuel Prices. Above $2 Mutuel Prices, the chart states "Official Program Numbers."

Marked Lady wore blinkers (b), carried 113 pounds, was eighth at the start, was fifth by two lengths at the 1/4 mark, fourth by one length at the halfway mark, second by half a length at the 3/4 mark, led in the stretch by one and a half lengths, then held on to win by a head.

To verify this, let's look at the call on Marked Lady at the bottom of the chart. "Marked Lady, never far back, rallied to catch Free Saint leaving the far turn and lasted over Tricky Tune in a long drive."

Free Saint, its stablemate, led into the far turn at the 3/4 mark, then faded badly to fifth. Tricky Turn, which was second, "made a run along the inside after entering the stretch but wasn't good enough in a stiff drive," according to the caller of the race.

This tells so much more about the horses than the cold line in the past performance charts. That's why they should be studied by the serious and astute bettors.

Other information about Marked Lady. Her jockey was N. Santagata, and the odds were 5.90-1, a little below 6-1. The horse is a bay filly by Singh (sire) and Miss Marked (dam) by Raise A Cup (the dam's sire). The trainer is Stephen Schaeffer. The owner is R. Spiegel.

We should know that daily double betting is allowed at the track, which means making one bet to pick the winners of both the first and second races. After the second race we see that a $2 daily double bet on the winners 2 and 2 (program numbered horses) paid $133.80.

There was Quinella betting in the second race, and the first and second finishers were numbers 2 and 8, and that paid $40.80. In Quinella betting, the two numbers you select have to finish first and second, in any order, for you to win your bet.

In the third race, there was Exacta betting, and the Exacta, 7-6, paid $30.20. In an Exacta bet, you must pick the correct numbers, which in this case were 7 and 6. If 6 won, you wouldn't win your bet, which would be the case in a Quinella.

Sometimes there is Quinella and Exacta betting in one race, as in the fourth race, with the Quinella of 7-9 paying $37.00, while the more difficult Exacta paid $90.40 to those bettors picking the exact order of finish in the race, 9 and 7.

Study the races shown on these charts to familiarize yourself with the official racing charts, so that you can read them intelligently. They supply invaluable information which shouldn't be disregarded by an astute bettor.

VIII. Handicapping A Race

Handicapping, or attempting to pick a winner of a race by an examination of the past performances of the horses in the race, is not an exact science. There are a number of unknown factors, the most important being the condition of the horse on the day of the race. If you're at the track, you can go down to the paddock where the horses are saddled up and look at the horse you want to bet on. But if you're at the OTB office or at a race book, you can't do that.

Even an examination of the horse itself might not tell you much. Thoroughbreds are sleek, powerful animals, bred and built for speed. They are beautiful beasts, but in a race they're all thoroughbreds and all might look good. So, eventually, it's the past performance charts that we must study to find a winner.

The following factors have been suggested by experts and pros at handicapping as important points to note when picking a winner.

1. Study the speed ratings. The horses with the best speed ratings in the race, or second-best, are more consistent winners than horses with lower speed ratings, particularly in sprint races.

2. Look for consistency. Good horses are consistent, and pay particular note to a horse who has been *knocking at the door*, that is, coming in 3rd or second in its last starts. This horse is in shape, and can win.

3. Always give strict attention to a horse that won the last time out, because this horse may be in prime condition and ready to repeat, particularly if it's running in the same class of race against horses it can beat.

4. Pay attention to class. A horse moving up in class is at a big disadvantage, and many false favorites are horses that have won against poorer company and look good on paper, but can't hold their own against better horses.

The easiest way to see this is to study the past performance charts. A horse moving from a claiming to an allowance race is really going in over its head most of the time, as is a horse going from a lower allowance race purse to a higher one. Just examining any past performance charts will show a graveyard of past winners who then finished out of the money when moving up this way.

5. Avoid horses that haven't raced in a long time. They often *need a race* as the handicappers say, to *tighten up*. If a horse hasn't raced in several months, be careful about betting it.

50

6. Always pay particular attention to beaten favorites the last time out. If they're still being heavily bet, then they are still in top condition. But a beaten favorite last time out who goes off at more than 4-1 is not a good bet. Horses are, for the most part, carefully trained to reach a peak performance, but they generally can't hold that peak for more than a few races, unless they're absolutely top class horses. You must catch the horse during these peak periods to make your score.

7. On off days, when the track is muddy or sloppy, look for horses that break fast out of the gate and can take an early lead. They stand a good chance of going all the way, because the horses behind them will be at a disadvantage with mud in their faces.

8. In fact, it's a good idea to study horses that can break fast and stay first, second or third at the first couple of calls. These horses win more than their share of races.

9. Watch the betting patterns at the track. If a horse is heavily bet down at the last few ticks of the tote board, then "smart money" is coming in. Often this horse, if he didn't figure before on past performance, will run at least third, but might not win the race.

10. If you're at the track, go to the paddock and look at the horses. Avoid those with their ears flat on their heads, or who look frightened, with their heads and eyes lolling about. They're usually bad bets to win the race.

No matter how strong or speedy a horse is, he still must be guided by a competent jockey in order to be a factor in the race. Like all athletes, jockeys run the gamut from the very best to incompetent. A poor jockey can hurt a good horse's chances at winning; a great jockey can help a good horse to win. However, horses that are weak and have no speed cannot be helped by the greatest of jockeys.

Some jockeys, such as Angel Cordero or Willie Shoemaker, have the ability to alter the odds on any horse they ride because of their outstanding skills, and jockeys such as these are such dominant figures that their skills are as important a factor in a big race as is the horse's past performance.

If in doubt, better to go with a *hot* jockey, one who has had a top winning record at the track. This kind of jockey attracts the best horses, and generally has an astute agent who picks winning horses for him.

Above all, find out as much information as you can about the horses you're betting on. And until you feel that you're a good handicapper, bet for fun, and bet the minimum. If you're out at the track, enjoy the day, but don't go overboard and risk too much money. And, of course, if you will be hurt financially or emotionally by betting on horses, don't bet. Only gamble with money you can afford to lose. This is important, don't forget it.

And good luck!!!!

IX. More Winning Tips

Horseracing presents a multitude of variants for the bettor, and this makes picking winners a complex business, even for the experienced and sophisticated bettor. First of all, a field will consist of a number of horses, up to 12 betting choices. Some of these horses will have had recent good races under their belts; others will have had recent poor showings.

Then there is the factor of distance. Some horses will have raced frequently at the distance of the race; others will wither be moving up to the distance and still others will find this a shorter race to contend with. Then there's the track condition, whether it be sloppy, muddy, good or fast. And each track has different soil and different racing conditions.

Often a racegoer will have to handicap a race of 1-1/8 miles in Santa Anita, a fast track, featuring horses that have run in slower times in Arlington Park or Aqueduct. Or some of the horses have done terrifically well at a distance of 6 and 7 furlongs and now are extending their stamina to be tested at the longer distance. A couple of the horses will be moving up in class, and a few moving down in class. The track condition is rated as a "good" for this race.

How can an average racegoer put all these factors into a blender and come up with a winner?

To become a winner at the racetrack, the bettor

must be in a position to handicap each race and select the horse that will win this race. It sounds easier than it is in real life.

There will be many races in which the bettor will face imponderables, in which selecting a winning horse will be like walking through a maze blindfolded. What should the racegoer do in this situation?

He should simply lay off the race and not bet it. The worst thing he can do is throw money away on a race that he or she can't figure out.

Often, ignorant bettors simply look up at the tote board and select the favorite and bet it. Their reasoning is as follows: "I can't figure this race out, but the money is on the 4 horse, and he's a 5-2 favorite. So I"ll simply bet the favorite. He should win, after all he's the favorite."

This is delusional thinking. The bettor thinking this way doesn't realize that thousands of other people at the track have the same thoughts, and thus the ignorant combine with the ignorant to send off a horse as a favorite just because they don't know what else to do.

Favorites win only 34% of the time, and that goes for all favorites at American race tracks. Odds-on favorites, those paying less than even-money to win, will come in for the bettor about 55% of the time. The percentages decrease as the odds go up for favorites.

Thus, you can be sure that even-money choices, going off at 1-1, will win more than 8-5 favorites, who will win more than 5-2 favorites. If favorites of all kinds win only 34% of the time, that means that they'll lose 66% of the time. And 5-2 favorites will be lucky to win much less of the time.

Blindly betting favorites is a sure way to lose money at the track. Not only won't you win, but when you do the payoffs will be small, and you'll miss the opportunity to make big money by betting horses that pay 5-1 or more, where you really start collecting serious money for your wager.

So we come back to handicapping the race, and we must remember that each race presents us with different conditions and different horses, and thus each race must be studied as a separate entity. If you can't properly handicap races, you shouldn't bet money at the track, because the only reason to bet is to win.

Sure, you might say, I'll go to the track and have some fun and wager a few bucks and yell myself hoarse for the horse I've backed. Fine and good. So long as you can afford to lose, and you limit yourself to the few bucks.

But nine races are involved, and often, the bettor who just wants to wager a few bucks, finds himself losing about $30 after several races and now starts to make big bets to try and win it back all at once, and then suddenly finds himself in a big hole, losing money he can't afford to lose. The fun aspect has left. If you don't think this is so, just look at the faces of the people leaving the racetrack after the last race.

No, the fun is in winning, and all the information presented in this book gives you the tools to win.

I would suggest that you first limit yourself to handicapping races at home by purchasing the Racing Form the night before and studying each race and picking a winner. Then go to the track the next day, cut out and eliminate all those horses that have been scratched (removed from the race by their trainers or owners) and watch how the betting goes.

Betting is important, for often there is a clue to where the "smart money" is going. By smart money, we mean money bet heavily by those who have inside information on the race.

Generally, this inside information relates to the condition of a particular racehorse, which the insiders feel can win the race.

They may know this from a variety of factors. They may have seen secret workouts where the horse has shown exceptional speed. Or they may have watched the horse steadily improve, without rushing the horse in previous races, so that his record looks mediocre, but now he's fit for this race and ready to win.

Let's now differentiate smart money from stupid money bet on a horse. The stupid pattern usually is as follows: the track handicapper has made the 7 horse the favorite on the morning line at 5-2. Money is bet on him as the favorite and five minutes before post time, he's 9-5. He goes up to 2-1 and then back down to 9-5, and in the last minute he drops to 8-5.

The vast majority of bettors think that "smart money" has dropped the odds on this horse at the last minute, but what really has happened is that thousands of bettors, unable to determine which horse will win, blindly bet on the favorite at the last minute. Then they watch him lose and tear up their tickets.

Here's how smart money operates. A horse opens in the morning line at 5-1, gets bet down to 4-1 with five minutes to go, then goes down to 7-2 with three minutes to go, and then with each tick on the tote board, drops, to 5-2, 2-1 and then finally goes off at 9-5.

Heavy money is going on this horse and not from the general betting public either. Insiders are betting that this horse can win. He might not win, but you can be sure he has a top chance at winning, and this sort of favorite, or second choice is well worth your bet. Often, it's good to bet this horse across the board, for if he doesn't win, there's a solid chance he'll place or show.

Inside bettors know that this horse is in fine condition. In each race you handicap, you must be sure that your selection is in this fine condition and stands a chance of winning. How will you know? If he has rounded into top shape, finishing fifth, then third, then just missing by a length at second, there is a good chance that he can win this time out. He has been "knocking on the door," as the handicappers say.

A horse that hasn't run for awhile, but has two good races under his belt, running fourth and third, evenly, but has shown good workouts recently, may be due to win. In this case watch the betting patterns closely. If late money comes on this horse, bet him also.

Another thing to look out for is class. Class is represented by the company the horse runs in. If it's a Grade A Stake horse, running in top races like the Kentucky Derby, the horse is of the best class. At the bottom are cheap claimers, running to be claimed for hundreds of dollars. At major race tracks, there will be horses moving up and down in class ever day.

For example, a horse that has run in Allowance races will drop down to a claiming race. Or a horse running as a $15,000 claimer, will move up to a $25,000 claim race. As a general rule, anytime a horse moves down in class, you must give this horse your undivided attention. You may end up not liking him, but you can't just dismiss the horse.

Suppose a horse has moved down in class, unable to compete with better horses, but now is in with cheap claimers. He has finished 8th, 9th and 6th with better company. He is established on the morning line at 8-1, is 6-1 with five minutes to go, and as you look up at the last minute, it goes off at 9-2.

Get some money on this animal. It may not win, but smart money feels it can win, and it may now be in fine condition to do so. You'll have a live animal in the race.

On the other hand, if this same horse, listed at 8-1, goes to 7-1, maybe 6-1, with five minutes to go, but then moves up again to 8-1, and goes off at 10-1, there's no inside money on him. This may not be his day to win. Avoid that horse.

What we're suggesting is to handicap your race the night before, not at the track, so you'll have more time to study the Form, and combine the handicapping with the betting patterns at the track. Both must be taken into consideration.

The thing is, concentrate on each race, then each type of race, and see which you can handicap correctly. If you become a whiz only at distance races of one mile or more, bet them and only them. Don't gamble too much. Don't go to the track to bet on every race. Pick your spots. The most fun anyone can have at the races is to leave with a wallet bulging with cash.

As we showed, there are a multitude of factors. You must eliminate them and concentrate on those factors that you know brings in winners, such as smart money patterns, fine conditions of the horses you bet, horses that outclass the others and so forth.

As you study the Racing Form, your feel for each race will improve. Be patient. Study and handicap, and only when you can win on paper, should you bet. You should be patient at the track and make sure your methods work. Don't just throw money away when you're unsure. And don't bet every race.

It may be difficult to figure out a winning pattern. After all, 95% of horse bettors are losers. But with the knowledge you've gained from this book, and with careful study, you might find a way to consistently win. Then, it will all pay off for you in solid profits.

2 FOR 1 OFFER!
The GRI Horseracing Super Strategies!

It took a long time to acquire these **time-tested** winning strategies - **must-buys** for serious horse players and now they're together in one **powerful** package - two $50.00 strategies selling for the price of one!

PIMLICO PHIL'S HANDICAPPING SECRETS

Here it is! Pimlico Phil has finally **revealed**, for the **first time**, and to GRI **exclusively**, his **winning secrets** on how to beat the track! Now that this **legendary** figure has retired, you too can win with these **powerful secrets!**

FIVE KEY FACTORS - Pimlico Phil found that, over the years, particular factors stood out above others in picking winners over and over again, and he has isolated the **five key factors** of winning at the track.

You'll learn which horse is the best bet on an off track and which horse gives you the best chances in a distance race. You'll learn how to analyze the fitness of the horse, the condition of the track, past performances, class of race and much, much more in this **brilliant compendium** of how to **win!**

EASY TO LEARN, SIMPLE TO USE - Pimlico Phil's **step by step** strategy is **simple to learn** and **powerful** and shows you how to analyze the important elements in a race, and how to translate that information into **winners!**

Jerry Einstein's: THE WHIZ KID SYSTEM

After analyzing the results of thousands of races, Jerry "The Whiz Kid" Einstein, has **at last** released **exclusively** to GRI, his **new**, **powerful** strategy for winning at the races - "The Whiz Kid System."

PLAY WITH THE ODDS! - The Whiz Kid System is a pure money play in which the mutuel odds are the predominant factor in picking winners, and **you'll be picking winners** with this method, day after day, week after week and year after year. You'll soon be **cherry-picking the best races!**

BE A WINNER! - The Whiz Kid System shows you how to play the percentages, how to pick winners and how to avoid losers. Armed with this **time-tested** strategy, lesser players will look up to you in awe!.

BONUS AND EXTRA BONUS!!! - Rush in an order now and you'll **receive both** strategies for only $50!!! (save $50), plus, **absolutely free,** "Five Extra Winning Tips" ($10 value), **inside info** from (GRI's) professional affiliates!

To order send $50 by bank check or money order to:

Cardoza Publishing, P.O. Box 1500, Cooper Station, New York, NY 10276
Please include $2.00 postage and handling for U.S. and Canadian orders, 4x for European orders and 6x for all other countries.

2 for 1 Offer!!!

Yes! I want to take advantage of this **2 for 1** offer. (Valid only with coupon)
Please *rush* me the Super Strategies plus the bonus, "5 Extra Winning Tips!"
Enclosed is a check or money order payable to Cardoza Publishing for $50.

NAME _____

ADDRESS _____

CITY _____ STATE _____ ZIP _____

Thoroughbred Horseracing Level I

Prof. Jones Software - (Available in IBM, Apple, Mac, C/64, TRS)

This powerful and easy-to-use program evaluates all the relevant factors of winning, calculates the information and prints out an accurate prediction of the winning horses in both charts and graphics! The Level I is designed for those individuals who go to the track a couple of times a month and has an average win % of the top pick of 40-43%!

EASY TO USE - FAST RESULTS - You enter the important information in the Update section - the latest track, jockey and trainer stats - then simply press the single-key command to analyze the race and give you the predicted winners and order of finish!

This package includes the CONFIGURATION MODULE, which configures the system to your computer, i.e. number of drives, printer used etc., and the ENTER MODULE - all input data can be found on the racing form and is entered in order on the Single Screen input.

QUESTIONS ASKED:

Name	Track Last	Time at 1/2	U/D/S class
Jockey Today	Distance Last	Time at Finish	Best Speed
Trainer Today	Distance at 1/4	Post Last	Date Last
Best Variance	Distance at 1/2	Speed Last	Workout Con.
Time at 1/4	Variance Last	Top 3 2nd Call	Wild Card
Distance behind at finish		1sts/2nds/3rds/Purses	

POWERHOUSE PROGRAM - This powerhouse program comes complete with easy-to-read hardbound manual and step-by-step instructions.

AFTER-PURCHASE SUPPORT - All Prof. Jones software packages have complete 90 day after-purchase support, 90 day replacement warranty (and optional 1 year extension) and are backed by 7 years of satisfied customers!

MANY MORE FEATURES - This incredible program includes full race analysis, help functions, single screen input!, "In Order" questions from the racing form, numeric racing chart, horse bar graph, comparison chart and much, much more - too much to list here.

To order, send $149.95 by bank check or money order to:
Cardoza Publishing, P.O. Box 1500, Cooper Station, New York, NY 10276
MC/Visa orders by phone (718)743-5229
Please include $3.00 postage and handling for U.S. and Canadian orders, 4x for European orders and 6x for all other countries.

Beat the Track!!!

I'm ready to be a winner! Please *rush* me Prof. Jones Thoroughbred Level I plus all the built-in features. Enclosed is a check or money order payable to Cardoza Publishing for $149.95.

NAME _____ Computer _____

ADDRESS _____

CITY _____ STATE _____ ZIP _____

Thoroughbred Horseracing Level II

Prof. Jones Software - (Available in IBM, Apple, Mac, C/64, TRS)

Level II is designed for the handicapper who desires a **higher winning percentage** and **complete betting analysis**. Designed for players who go to the track once a week or more, this **very powerful** program has **all the goodies** of Level I plus -

Expanded Modules - The Update Module compensates for late scratches and holds 50 sets of track, jockeys and trainer records! An expanded track configuration uses a Post Bias for assigning different weights to different post positions.

More Features - The advanced Fractional Adjustor gives accurate early speed and closing abilities of each animal regardless of distance. Post Bias is also evaluated for both sprint and route, while the Master Bettor˜ shows the exact bet, horse and type of bet recommended.

And More Features - There's much more to this powerful package - The Level II not only provides an on-screen betting philosophy and a Horse Watch List - but additionally, a Pro Series Money Management strategy!

POWERHOUSE PROGRAM - This Level II comes complete with step-by-step instructions, software and easy-to-read hardbound manuals, along with the standard full-service support!

If you're a serious horseplayer - order your package now! For beginning and intermediate players, the Level II will get you winning at the track!

AFTER-PURCHASE SUPPORT - All Prof. Jones software packages have complete 90 day after-purchase support, 90 day replacement warranty (and optional 1 year extension) and are backed by 7 years of satisfied customers!

UPDATE MODULE

50 sets of track records, 50 jockeys, and 50 trainers records.
Compensates for late scratches.

ANALYSIS/OUTPUT MODULE

Single key command to analyze race.
Results of analysis shown on screen and/or printed on paper.
Output shown using Charts and Graphs for visual clarity.

ENTER MODULE

Single Screen Input.
All input data can be found on the Racing Form, and is entered in order.

To order, send $249.95 by bank check or money order to:
Cardoza Publishing, P.O. Box 1500, Cooper Station, New York, NY 10276
MC/Visa Orders at (718)743-5229

Please include $3.00 postage and handling for U.S. and Canadian orders, 4x for European orders and 6x for all other countries.

I'm ready to be a winner! Please *rush* me Prof. Jones Thoroughbred Level II plus all the built in features. Enclosed is a check or money order payable to Cardoza Publishing for $249.95 (plus postage and handling).

NAME _____ Computer _____

ADDRESS _____

CITY _____ STATE _____ ZIP _____

Greyhound Level I and Level II

Prof. Jones Software - (Available in IBM, Apple, Mac, C/64, TRS)

Greyhound Level I

This Professional Series basic race analysis program is targeted to individuals who go to the track a couple of times each month, want the latest in Prof. Jones software tools, but haven't yet felt the need for all the features of its big brother, Level II.

Many Winning Tools - Similar to the Level I Thoroughbred (see that ad) in the features, but targeted, of course to Greyhound betting. Complete race analysis, friendly "help" functions, single screen input, questions asked are "in order," update module holds 50 kennel records and one set of track records and many more features too numerous to list here.

Questions Asked:

Name	Kennel	1/8 Time	Actual Time
Track Condition	Track Condition Last	Distance Last	Best Speed
Winners Time	Post Last	Post	Running Style
1/8 at Higher Grade	2/More 1/8 Same Gd	Stretch	Finish
Grade/Grade Last	Starts/1sts/2nds/3rds	Wild Card	Distance

Greyhound Level II

Designed for the serious greyhound bettor who goes to the track about once a week, the Level II gives the handicapper higher win percentages and a complete betting analysis.

Features Galore! - This popular program gives you all the good stuff of the Thoroughbred Level II - the Configuration and Enter Modules, single screen input, Master Bettor , higher winning percentage capability, complete betting analysis, complete race analysis, Watch List, help functions, etc, except of course, this super strategy is designed specifically for the Greyhounds.

Versatile and Powerful - You'll thrill at this pro level program with extras like pro series Greyhound Money Management, expanded multiple track capacity, double check holding tanks, artificial track record capacity, betting modes, watch lists, on-screen betting philosophy and much, much more!

AFTER-PURCHASE SUPPORT - Includes complete 90 day after-purchase support, 90 day replacement warranty and optional 1 year extension. Backed by 7 years of satisfied customers! Easy-to-read hardbound manual included.

To order send $149.95 for Level I or $249.95 for Level II to:

Cardoza Publishing, P.O. Box 1500, Cooper Station, New York, NY 10276

MC/Visa orders at (718)743-5229

Please include $3.00 postage and handling for U.S. and Canadian orders, 4x for European orders and 6x for all other countries.

I'm ready to be a winner! Please *rush* me Prof. Jones Greyhound Level I ($149.95) or Level II ($249.95). Enclosed is a check or money order payable to Cardoza Publishing. (Please include postage and handling.)

NAME _____ Computer _____

ADDRESS _____

CITY _____ STATE _____ ZIP _____

HOW TO WIN AT HORSERACING!

A New Book by Robert V. Rowe

New and Exciting!!! A Must Buy!!!

At last, one of the great horseracing minds has put all his **winning knowledge** together in one easy-to-read and informative book! This **new and exciting** book by Robert V. Rowe, *Racing Action* columnist and former editor of *American Turf Monthly*, is one of the **best books** ever on how to beat the track. Here is his long awaited and definitive book. Here's what the critics say about this living legend!

"This is a great, honest book with tons of information. The most important horseracing book in years!" Whitney L. Cobb

"One of the best players I have ever known..." Al Illich

"[His...] selection method is by far the simplest and most sensible...[and] is logical...enough to fall well within the grasp of any player." Tom Ainslee

"Very interesting reading for all race goers and is well worth the price. Far better than any system costing double..." Philip's Racing Newsletter

Learn to Beat the Track Now!

Original Research Shows You How to Win! - Rowe's original research, including the most comprehensive survey of wagering trends ever undertaken, spans more than **45 years** and shows you how to **win at the track!** This **amazing winning method** is packed solid with real **inside information!**

A New Winning Approach! - You'll learn how to find the **unorthodox ways to win**, for as Rowe says, "If you are going to use the identical sources of information ...and approach handicapping...as most others, you will lose like most others." Learn how to avoid falling into the trap of "smart money." Rowe shows you the real ways of getting value for your bets.

27 Chapters and 93 Charts! - Learn how to spot "hot" and "cold" horses from betting trends, how to analyze and play winning favorites, bet-downs and profitable exactas, how to evaluate trainers, jockeys, stable entries; how to analyze finishing positions and past results, how to make your own odds-line, and much, much more in this fact-filled, important book!

Hardbound with Dust Jacket! - This edition is not available in stores.

To order, send just $24.95 (postage paid) by check or money order to:
Cardoza Publishing
P.O. Box 1500, Cooper Station, New York, NY 10276

Mail in Your Order Today!

Yes! I want to be a winner at horseracing! Please *rush* me Robert V. Rowe's *How to Win at Horseracing* Enclosed is a check or money order payable to Cardoza Publishing for $24.95.

NAME _____

ADDRESS _____

CITY _____ STATE _____ ZIP _____